YOGI
LAST GAME'S

A True Story About
Yogi Berra, Whitey Ford & Phil Rizzuto

A Pictorial Documentary

A major league baseball player may never know when he'll play his last game in the majors. Fighting in WWII during the invasion of Normandy, nineteen-year old Lawrence Peter "Yogi" Berra didn't know if he would survive to play again, let alone, when or where. When a player says this is my last game, it usually is. Yogi's last MLB game was not his last competitive game it was his next to last. Yogi Berra's Last Game documents the week, of September 12-18, 1994, with interviews and pictures that led up to Yogi Berra's last competitive game he played and managed in a Yankees uniform. This is the list of former MLB players who took part in this historical and unprecedented baseball game.

1.Yogi Berra - Catcher and Outfielder for NY Yankees 1946 -1965, Manager of Yankees and NY Mets, Hall of Fame member, All-Century Team Catcher, Presidential Medal of Freedom Recipient, Philosopher, Author.
2.Whitey Ford - Pitcher for NY Yankees 1950 - 1967, Hall of Fame member, All-Century Team Pitcher, Author.
3.Phil "Scooter" Rizzuto - Shortstop for N.Y. Yankees 1941-1956, Hall of Fame member, 40 years as Radio and Television announcer for the Yankees, Author.
4.Enos "Country" Slaughter - Right Fielder for Saint Louis Cardinals 1938 - 1953, N.Y. Yankees 1954, Kansas City Athletics 1955, NY Yankees 1956 -1959, Hall of Fame member.
5.Ralph Branca - Pitcher for Brooklyn Dodgers, Detroit Tigers, NY Yankees 1944 - 1956.
6.Bill White - First Baseman and Outfielder for New York and S.F. Giants, St. Louis Cardinals, Philadelphia Phillies 1956 - 1969, First Black National League President, Radio and Television announcer for NY Yankees.
7. Ron Leflore - Center Fielder for Detroit Tigers, Monteal Expos, Chicago White Sox 1974-1982.
8. Joe Pignatano - Catcher for Brooklyn and L.A. Dodgers, Kansas City Royals, Toronto Blue Jays, S.F.Giants, NY "Miracle" Mets 1957-1962
9. Del Alston - First Baseman and Outfielder for Yankees, Toronto Blue Jays, Oakland A's, Cleveland Indians 1977-1980

Yogi Berra's Last Game

While the 1994 MLB strike dragged on into September and the World Series was canceled, three of the greatest NY Yankees to ever play the game played their last game together.

Hall of Fame legends Yogi Berra, Whitey Ford and Phil "Scooter" Rizzuto flew from New York's JFK Airport to Vienna, Austria on September 11th, 1994 as ambassadors of America's Pastime. They came to promote baseball and play in the inaugural Austrian Cup exhibition game against the first Austrian All Stars players, who built the first baseball field, in the village of Stockerau near Vienna, Austria.

The days before the game, they were first introduced to the Mayor-elect of Vienna and presented him with an autographed bat, Yankees cap and uniform. The following day they received a private concert from the world-renowned Vienna Boys Choir. Yogi, Whitey and Scooter enjoyed the concert so much, they decided to share the game they loved and played baseball with these famous children on their soccer field. Yogi taught them to hit, Scooter taught them to bunt, and Whitey taught them to sing, "Take Me Out To The Ballgame." These immortal NY Yankees toured palaces and castles, in the days that followed, where many more comical, historical and unprecedented pictures of them were created, that New Yorkers and Americans need to see. Finally on Sunday, September 18th, 1994 they played Yogi Berra's last game, with an outcome they didn't expect.

This historical pictorial documentary includes over four hundred never before seen pictures of Yogi, Whitey, Scooter, their teammates and wives, along with never before heard transcribed conversations and quotes from hours of historical audiovisual footage. This magical week in baseball can finally be seen and read by Yankees fans, baseball fans and Americans for the first time. They were the shining light in the darkest days of baseball.

Table of Contents

VIENNA AIRPORT

Yogi stood at the Vienna airport baggage claim. He looked at me and pointed his finger. "Cecil B. DeMille," Yogi teased. A big grin appeared on his face. He'd been in front of a lot of cameras in his career. He was in the movie "That Touch of Mink" with Doris Day, Cary Grant, Mickey Mantle and Roger Maris. Oh yeah, and a record 75 World Series games!

Yogi Berra's Last Game

For those unfamiliar with Cecil B. DeMille he directed the classic film, "The Ten Commandments", starring Charlton Heston, Yul Brynner and Edward G. Robinson. The movie premiered Friday October 5, 1956. DeMille could be compared to the Steven Spielberg of Yogi's era and maybe the movie era Yogi was most familiar with.

Coincidently, on Friday October 5th 1956, Yankees catcher Yogi Berra hit a home run and four RBI'S in Game 2 of the World Series. Although the NY Yankees lost to the Brooklyn Dodgers at Ebbets Field 13-8, they won the series. I wonder if Yogi and his wife Carmen went to see The Ten Commandments after the game that night. He hit two more home runs in game seven for a score of 2-0 to clinch the series. On October 8th in Game 5 of the 1956 World Series, Yogi called and caught the first post-season perfect game (no-hitter) in World Series history that was pitched by Don Larsen. Hall of Fame legends Whitey Ford and Enos Slaughter, who went on this 1994 trip to Austria with Yogi, were also on the 1956 World Series Champion New York Yankees. Whitey won Game 3 and Enos hit a home run. Phil was released from the team August 25, 1956 and replaced by Enos for the postseason roster. Mantle and Berra both hit three home runs in the series.

> *It's the only time Yankees teammates and Hall of Fame legends Berra, Ford, Rizzuto and Slaughter were in Europe and it was their last game together.*

This game played in Austria is historically significant for baseball. It's the only time Yankees teammates and Hall of Fame legends Berra, Ford, Rizzuto and Slaughter were in Europe and it was their last game together.

On the flight from NYC to Vienna Phil asked for a cap to wear, so I gave him my Yankees cap. I approached him while he waited for his luggage at baggage claim. When he saw me he immediately thanked me.

"I got your hat! I wore this the whole way... it really helped me," Phil "Scooter" Rizzuto said. The voice of the Yankees for forty years spent his entire thirteen year baseball career as Yankees shortstop. "The Scooter" had been inducted to the Baseball Hall of Fame on July 31st, just before the 1994 MLB strike began on August 12th.

Yogi, Whitey and their wives Carmen and Joan pushed their baggage carts from the Vienna airport terminal. They resembled any other tourists on vacation. "Why buy good luggage, you only use it when you travel,"Yogi once said. The difference is that these tourists own sixteen World Series rings between them. Yogi won a record ten rings and Whitey won six, which is the record for MLB pitchers.

Yogi Berra's Last Game

"Went off the curb," Yogi joked, after he wrestled the cart from tipping over. Yogi has also been heard to say. "It ain't over, till it's over."

Phil, who is the winner of eight World Series rings, and his wife Cora walked from the airport terminal pushing their baggage cart and waved.

"Hi mom!" Phil exclaimed, as he wore the only MLB franchise logo he had ever worked for in over forty years.

"How was your flight?" I asked, as he walked up to me.

"The finest overseas trip I've ever had... it's the only one I've ever had... but it's the first time I slept on a plane in my whole life. Never slept on any plane that the Yankees were on or anything," Phil replied, with broadcaster spontaneity. He pondered for a moment and recalled his experience with the pilot. "I was sitting up front with the pilot but they wouldn't let me take the microphone. I wanted to say let's have a hand for the Scooter landing his two thousandth plane but the pilot wouldn't let me... I don't think he understood me... he could hardly talk English," Phil teased. "He let me sit right next to him watching the landing. Went over the Blue Danube ...saw the Austrian Alps. They don't compare with our Rockies... but you know... they were nice little hills.

"I wanted to say let's have a hand for the Scooter landing his two thousandth plane but the pilot wouldn't let me... I don't think he understood me..."

Yogi was arranging his luggage when I walked up to him.

"How was your flight?" I asked, hoping to hear him reply with if a new "Yogi-ism."

"Good Flight," Yogi replied.

"Did you sleep?" I asked.

"On and off," Yogi replied.

It was 10:00 AM in Vienna when he figured out the time back in New York.

"Six hours different! 4 o'clock," Yogi said, as he rolled his eyes knowing he'd still be sleeping back home. Yogi still had a sense of humor, after an eight-and-a-half hour flight, with a camera pointed in his face.

Yogi Berra's Last Game

Phil was handed a baseball bat which he tossed onto the luggage. "That's not my model," the Yankees shortstop joked. He bent down and picked the bat from the luggage. "All the good hitters use thin handle bats... makes them whip the bat," Phil remarked. He pointed to a spot on the bat. "But yah got to be a good hitter because I hit a lot between here and here and I splintered a bat." Phil "Scooter" Rizzuto is, regarded as one of the best bunters in baseball history. As a Yankees shortstop his 1,217 career double plays ranks 17th in major league history in 13 years played. Derek Jeter is 6th with 20 years played and will be the next Yankees shortstop inducted into the Hall of Fame.

Yogi Berra's Last Game

He played his first major league game on April 14, 1941. Phil was named the American Leagues Most Valuable Player in 1950. That year he hit .324 with 200 hits, 92 walks and scored 125 runs. He led all hitters in the 1942 World Series with a .381 average. He served in the United States Navy from 1943 through 1945 during World War II. In 1994 he was inducted into the Hall of Fame. Phil looked at the crowd in front of him. "I'm playing in the game! Did you see the list of the other guys? Boy 'll tell yah... they gonna throw them in and tire us out like a football game! There's some American names in there... did yah notice?" Phil remarked. "Well you look at it... there's a couple of ringers!"

"Hans Smith!" someone in the crowd exclaimed. Phil laughed.

Yogi Berra's Last Game

Chapter 2

YOGI AND THE MAYOR

The next morning everyone passed the time on the sidewalk in front of the Hotel before they got on the bus to meet the Mayor-elect of Vienna.

Whitey Ford walked toward the bus and turned to me.

"Hold it," Whitey said. He stopped with a suit jacket over his shoulder and a baseball logo tie on his crisp pink shirt. He pulled his jacket on and opened the lapel to reveal an inner lining with logos of baseball teams.

"Line up all the pitchers in the world in front of me, and give me first choice, and I'd pick Whitey," said Mickey Mantle.

"If you had one game to win and your life depended on it, you'd want Ford to pitch it," said Casey Stengel.

Yogi also wore his baseball logo tie when he arrived outside the hotel.

"I was gonna bring mine you know... but I said... well I don't know... It might be too flashy over there." Enos Slaughter remarked.

"Fancy boy," Joe Pignatano teased. Joe was a World Series catcher for the 1959 Los Angeles Dodgers and a Mets coach after his playing career. Four time Super Bowl referee Tony Veteri stood beside them. Yogi grinned as he looked at the tie Joe wore, which had cartoon characters on it.

Phil came out of the hotel and stood beside Joe, who quietly told Phil a story so it couldn't easily be heard. From Phil's response it must have been funny.

"No way!" Phil exclaimed, as he laughed.

"We laughed like hell... I tell yah," Joe said. Phil looked up and saw the boom microphone hovering above his head.

"Hey!" Phil exclaimed, as he cleared his throat.

"Evidently she was a G.I.'s wife," Joe said, as he finished telling his story.

"Oh yeah!" Phil exclaimed as he laughed.

Yogi Berra's Last Game

"Be careful what you say," some of their wives in the crowd said to Phil.

"Yeah... I see that," Phil replied.

"Hey... they can delete," Joe replied. The wives giggled.

"Candid Camera!" Phil exclaimed. He stood looking about for a moment. "What a beautiful day! I wanta tell yah something... I never slept better in my life! Whitey kept feeding me those Grand Marnier's."

"That's a good drink," Joe remarked.

"Holy Cow!" Phil exclaimed.

Everyone boarded the bus to meet the Mayor of Vienna.

"We're going to see the Mayor... and not Giuliani," Dell Alston joked. Dell been an outfielder for the NY Yankees, Cleveland Indians and the Oakland Athletics.

When they got to their destination Yogi and Ralph Branca assisted the ladies off the bus.

"Come on Nancy...jump," Yogi teased. Nancy Pignatano, Joe's wife, giggled as she stepped onto the sidewalk.

Whitey waved and grinned at me as a lady walked past him. He was the premier NY Yankees pitcher of his time and recorded ten World Series pitching victories. Roger Maris broke Babe Ruth's single season home run record in 1961. Whitey broke Babe Ruth's record in 1961 for pitching 29 2/3 consecutive scoreless innings in the World Series that the Babe held for 43 years. Whitey holds the World Series scoreless streak at 33 2/3 innings.

"It was a bad year for the Babe," Whitey joked. Whitey's overall winning percentage of .690 stands as the best in baseball's modern era. When Ford retired from the game in 1967, he left as the standard-bearer in many World Series pitching categories. To this day, Ford still holds records for the Fall Classic with most wins (10), innings pitched (146), games started (22) and strikeouts (94). Whitey is known as "The Chairman of the Board" for the way he controlled the game. He won 236 games. He won the most in Yankees history.

Yogi Berra's Last Game

Yogi finally caught up to Whitey as they walked toward the Belvedere Palace, which is a complex of two palaces and extensive gardens. During the Napoleonic Wars, Vienna was taken by Napoleon twice, in 1805 and 1809.

"Even Napoleon had his Watergate," Yogi once said.

"There's a big swimming pool," Yogi joked to Whitey as they walked past a large pool of water on the palace grounds.

"Hey is that a swimming pool?" Yogi jokingly asked the tour guide.

"This was the summer residence," the tour guide replied as she smiled maintaining her professionalism.

"Not to shabby," Yogi said as he laughed.

Yogi Berra's Last Game

"I had cheerios and fruit... that's all I had. Cheerios and fruit... and about eight cups of coffee," Phil commented as he followed Cora, while she took pictures of the Palace and gardens. "This is something... isn't it," Phil remarked.

A short time later Yogi, Whitey, Phil and Joe gathered to pose for a photo. Brooklyn Dodgers pitching legend Ralph Branca, who pitched five games for the Yankees in 1954, walked over to get in the picture.

"Hey White!" Phil shouted, as he gestured to his old Yankees games broadcast partner to get in the picture with them. "Oh... I heard what he said!" Phil exclaimed to Yogi. "Did you hear what he said?"

"What?" Yogi asked.

"They're all Italian," Phil said. "Whitey's here." Yogi and his former Yankees teammates laughed. Hall of Fame player Enos "Country" Slaughter, who played outfield for the Yankees starting in 1956, walked over and stood with the guys to be photographed.

"Fire at will!" Enos ordered militarily. "Take some more!"

23

"Don't stand by Slaughter he'll hit yah one!" Phil shouted.

"You didn't invite him to dinner last night," Yogi teased.

"Don't take any side shots!" Phil shouted. "No profile shots!"

"Now this will be in the Post Office next week... right!" Joe shouted.

They all laughed at the thought of themselves on a wanted poster in the Post Office. Their camaraderie as former Yankees was enduring.

"They got all the girls over there," Yogi whispered to Whitey as they hung out and observed the crowd.

"I know that!" Whitey replied. "Five girls... but none of them are blondes!" Yogi clapped his hands together and laughed hysterically. You can't take the young man out of old Hall of Fame Yankees teammate.

"Do you remember 1955?" the tour guide to asked Yogi and Whitey.

"Yeah... I do," Yogi replied. The Brooklyn Dodgers defeated the NY

Yogi Berra's Last Game

Yankees in the 1955 World Series. Jackie Robinson stole home in Game 1 against catcher Yogi Berra and pitcher Whitey Ford on September 28th. The Yankees and Whitey won Game 1. The play became one of the most famous in World Series history. Yogi still says, "Yer out!"

"Yeah... we read about it," someone in the group shouted jokingly.

NY Yankees Royalty was walking through this royal palace. Shortly after people were talking and not listening to the tour guide.

"Shh!" Yogi whispered.

"It was impossible to get a conversation going, everybody was talking too much," Yogi once said. He continued listening to the tour guide speak.

Yogi Berra's Last Game

They finally arrived, after a short bus ride, at the entrance of Vienna City Hall to meet the Mayor-elect and walked inside.

The Vienna City Hall was designed by Friedrich Schmidt and erected between 1872 and 1883. It was built with a tower similar to gothic cathedrals. Today the City Hall is is the head office of Vienna's municipal administration with more than 2000 people working there. The magnificent state rooms are frequently used for events such as concerts, balls and Hall of Fame baseball players.

"Oh, oh... don't tell me we have to go up these steps!" Phil exclaimed as Yogi guided him with his hand up the staircase.

"Why... can't you make it?" Yogi asked as they stepped inside to climb the long steep staircase.

"I do this every morning," Yogi said with a grin at the top of the stairs.

They entered an official state room to meet the Mayor-elect and the

Yogi Berra's Last Game

young Austrian baseball players they would compete against in a few days.

On November 24, 2015, Yogi was awarded the Presidential Medal of Freedom posthumously by President Barack Obama in a ceremony at the White House. Obama used one of Berra's famous 'Yogi-isms', saying, "One thing we know for sure, If you can't imitate him, don't copy him." Yogi met every president since Harry Truman except Obama.

The Mayor arrived and gave a short speech through a translator.

"I want to give you a warm welcome to Vienna. I'm aware that among you we find some of the greatest and most famous athletes in the United States. Thank you for coming and all the best to you!" the Mayor-elect exclaimed.

When Yogi met Pope John XXIII in 1959 a reporter asked if he had an audience with him, Yogi replied "No, but I saw him. You know, he must read the papers a lot, because he said, "Hello Yogi."

"And what did you say?" asked the reporter.

"I said, Hello, Pope," replied Yogi.

Phil stepped up to the front of the room to give his speech to the Mayor. There were portraits of former Austrian dignitaries, the American flag and his Yankees teammates watching to hear what he would say.

"We are very, very happy and excited to be here. We're also very happy to be here to get baseball more notoriety. We have a lot of things to give to the Mayor. This baseball bat is just one we'd like to present to him... the only thing is... I see all those young coats down there that we gotta play against on Sunday and we're a little scared... but we'll try our best!" Phil exclaimed. "And where's the Mayor?"

Yogi Berra's Last Game

Phil presented the Mayor with an autographed Louisville Slugger.

Yogi and the Mayor were laughing as he stepped up and presented him with the Yankees road gray uniform.

"Speech!" someone in the crowd shouted to Yogi as he held the uniform.

"Who me?" Yogi asked, as if they were crazy. "I can't make a speech. What speech?"

"Speech!" someone shouted again.

"Yeah sure," Yogi replied. His speeches were heartfelt even when they didn't go so well. You knew what he meant, even when they were hard to understand. "I wanna thank everyone for making this night necessary," Yogi said June 6, 1947, during "Yogi Berra Night" in St. Louis.

Del stood between Yogi and the Mayor signing his autograph on the bat. While avoiding the speech everyone tried to persuade Yogi to give, Del stuck the top of the bat into Yogi's face like a microphone to speak into when he wasn't looking. Yogi turned his head and barely avoided being hit in the face with the bat as the Mayor reached for the uniform.

Yogi Berra's Last Game

"He'd fall in a sewer and come up with a gold watch," said Yankees Manager Casey Stengel, about the luck of Yogi Berra.

Yogi grinned and watched the Mayor proudly model his Yankees uniform as he reached for the bat to autograph.

Yogi laughed as he waited to autograph another bat Phil was signing.

"Oh... it's beautiful!" Phil exclaimed as the Mayor presented him with a memento "Thank you very much. Oh... this is wonderful... I'll treasure this!" Whitey stood quietly in the back avoiding any official duties.

The Mayor held the the autograpged bat Yogi presented to him and tried to pronounce a name on it. "Enos..." the Mayor mumbled. Yogi looked at the Mayor and they both laughed at his pronunciation of Enos Slaughter's name.

Yogi Berra's Last Game

He pointed at the Mayor. "You'd rather play soccer," Yogi said with a grin.

"Cricket!" someone in the crowd shouted.

"Yeah," Yogi replied as he and the Mayor laughed.

Yogi Berra's life is somewhat similar to the life of the fictional character Forest Gump. They weren't educated, both served in the military and had successful careers, that seemingly fell into their laps.

A short time later as the festivities continued, Yogi stood beside the Mayor and posed for another group photo with him.

"Look at all the girls," Yogi remarked to the Mayor who laughed, although he didn't understand English. The usual barrage of camera flashes went off. "Got it all?" Berra's ambassadorial efforts for baseball were a homerun. Yogi made everyone smile, except opposing pitchers.

When nobody responded the group scattered but Ralph Branca took the opportunity and microphone to say a few words to the Mayor.

"We want to thank the Mayor for having us... danke schon. Good luck in your new term from all of us.. lot's of luck... as a Mayor you'll need it." Ralph joked. The Mayor smiled at Ralph's comment and began to laugh once it was translated. A waiter approached Phil and Whitey with a tray of champagne and the festivities continued.

"Cora ...champagne!" he quietly exclaimed. Phil laughed at Whitey when he saw him take the glass of champagne and sniff it to assess the bouquet.

Yogi Berra's Last Game

Yogi grinned as he enjoyed a moment of conversation with Cora Rizzuto. Yogi and his wife Carmen didn't partake in the refreshments served.

Phil had a conversation with John Moore, Director of WPIX, about the Austrian baseball players as they enjoyed the festivities. .

"A kid was telling me... and he talks English very well." Phil explained to John. "And I asked him are we gonna play nine innings? He was telling me... don't you worry he says... there are four or five of the Austrian kids who are gonna play with us, against them, to help." John stood for a moment pretending to be puzzled while he came up with a response

"So, we're playing a double header?" John joked.

"No," Phil replied as he laughed. A few feet away Whitey and Cora talked while they enjoyed the champagne and festivities.

A short time later, Phil's assistant Anthony unintentionally stepped in front of a player's wife as she tried to take a group photo of Yogi, Ralph, Phil, Bill, and Whitey. Yogi pointed at him as they waited for the picture.

"Anthony... yah got right in front of Edna!" Phil shouted as he stood between Yogi and Bill. "Anthonyyyy!" they all chanted.

"Kick him Edna!" Whitey exclaimed as they all had a good laugh.

Yogi Berra's Last Game

A moment later, as they finally composed themselves, a classic picture of Yogi, Ralph, Phil, Bill and Whitey was taken. The guys in this picture are all highlighted in Ken Burns baseball documentary. Yogi had his own segment. Casy Stengel said of Yogi Berra, "I never play a game without my man." Stengel considered Yogi second only to Joe DiMaggio as the best players he ever managed. Yogi and Phil were on the Yankees team that won five consecutive World Series.

As the group disbanded a baseball was handed to Yogi and the others to autograph.

"Phil... sign the ball" Yogi ordered.

"Yes," Phil replied.

A short time later a young Austrian journalist interviewed Phil and

Yogi Berra's Last Game

asked about the MLB strike and World Series cancellation.

"They're making millions!" exclaimed Phil. "In those days, you could have no agent. You know what agents are? No agents... They could give you anything they wanted to give you. You had no minimum salary like they have today... which is great for the kids coming up... but the only thing that has done is brought on these strikes. There is no more baseball. It's terrible... absolutely terrible! The players and the owners... I have no sympathy for. They ruined... they ruined what could have been the greatest year for baseball ever! Because they were stubborn... there's no more baseball! They called off the World Series, which is really terrible... first time since 1904 that they haven't had the World Series. They had it when they had the war years, when they had the big collapse of the bridge in San Francisco and this year because of money... and they're both making so much! I can't... and the poor fans.

> *They called off the World Series, which is really terrible.*
> *First time since 1904 that they haven't had the World Series.*
> *They had it when they had the war years.*

The fans are the ones who get hurt the most... and the people who work trying to make a living," Phil remarked.

"Mr. Clinton was very," the Austrian journalist began to say.

"Ah... yes... well yes," Phil replied evasively, shaking his head. "It's a shame... it really is a shame... but that gave me an early vacation. I don't have to broadcast the games," Phil said.

"Free time?" the Journalist asked.

"Free time... yes," Phil replied.

"You finished your career in 1956... after this you started television... only for Yankees games?" the Journalist asked.

"I've been the longest ever with the Yankees continuously. I started with the Yankees in 1941 to 1956. I played sixteen years and this is my 38th year broadcasting the games. That's a total of 54 years that I've been with the Yankees continuously. Five years in a row, five Pennants, five World Series. Nobody's ever done that. Nobody will ever do it again... not the way it's set up now. The five in a row... 49, 50, 51, 52 and 53... but in all the time I was with the Yankees we won ten Pennants and eight World Series. Twice we lost the World Series, which is very unusual for the Yankees," Phil remarked.

Yogi and Bill came over to talk tothe young Austrian players with Phil. Phil asked an important question to the Austrain player, whom he thought was a pitcher. Bill seized the moment to tease Phil, while Yogi

Yogi Berra's Last Game

stood beside Phil listening and laughing.

"You have good control?" Phil asked the Austrian pitcher. The Austrian player just stood and smiled.

"Nobody's gonna hit yah," Bill White teased.

"What do you mean... nobody's gonna hit yah!" Phil exclaimed.

"Get out of the way," Bill teased. Yogi and Phil laughed at Bill's comment. "Watch the bunt," Bill said to the Austrian players as he demonstrated Phil's bunting technique.

"Don't tell them that! Phil exclaimed with a insincere grimace. "Will you stop it White!" The former Yankees shortstop was a famously casual broadcaster, who left games in the seventh inning so he could beat the traffic home to New Jersey. Phil broadcast Yankees game with Bill White for 18 seasons and always called him "White," never "Bill."

"He can't run anymore though," Yogi teased.

"He can't hit either," Bill teased. "So all he's gonna do is bunt."

Yogi, Phil and Bill laughed like crazy.

"Oh! He's terrible!" Phil exclaimed as they all laughed. "The Scooter made it to the Hall of Fame in 1994 because he was a star, one of the most popular players of his day and an ambassador for the game. Phil could count his friends in the millions and few men, including ballplayers, can say that.

When the "Scooter" was dying in 2007, Bill White visited him in the hospital and silently held his hand. "I loved Phil Rizzuto." said Bill.

During the dsicussion Phil demonstrated with his hand where he wanted the pitch thrown. Yogi positioned his hand in the same manner.

"But just about right there... right there... ok," Phil instructed. "It's easy to bunt right there." Yogi grinned has he positioned his hand in the same manner. Phil without missing a beat moved his hand higher in front of his face, "Not here," he comically explained as Yogi watched him with a grin.

Yogi Berra's Last Game

He pointed to the side of his head. "Not here!" Phil exclaimed jokingly knowing the outcome of a pitch to the side of the head. Yogi bent slightly at the waste with laughter.

It's said, that the reason players don't leave their gloves on the field between innings started because of Phil. He carried his off the field for fear that someone would stick a spider in it when he wasn't looking.

"Who's the good hitter on your team?" Phil asked a young Austrain player.

"I can't play because my knee hurts." he replied.

"You can't play!" Phil exclaimed, as though he couldn't believe what he heard.

"My knee hurts too!" Bill teased.

"What'd he say?" Phil asked.

"He said his knee hurts," Bill replied.

"What do yah think we got? We got aches all over!" Phil exclaimed. "He's got one knee that hurts." Yogi and Bill laughed. "How do you like that," Phil teased.

"Why do we have to have an ugly announcer like you and they got her?" a guy in the crowd jokingly asked Phil.

"Oh... no kidding!" Phil exclaimed.

"She's an announcer," the guy said.

Yogi Berra's Last Game

"But if I had that hat I'd look good," Phil said as he noticed the hat she wore on her head.

"You want it?" the young lady asked.

"Yeah," Phil replied. Whitey laughed as he took the hat off the young woman's head and placed it on Phil's. Yogi pointed at the hat on Phil's head and cracked up laughing along with everyone else.

A short time later Yogi and Phil crouched for another group picture.

"Snap it!" Phil shouted. "Hurry up Cora snap it! Press the button!" Yogi started to laugh uncontrollably.

He laughed so hard he had to stand up just as the flash of the camera went off. "You can observe a lot by just watching." Yogi once said.

Yogi Berra's Last Game

Yogi got back into his crouch and by this time Phil's old shortstop legs must have been cramping from squatting so long. Yogi composed himself for the final photo attempt.

"Hurry up!" Phil shouted to his wife. "Snap it!"

Yogi and Phil played eleven years together for the NY Yankees. Yogi won the MVP in three of those years and Phil won it once. They played together on six World Series winning teams and both are in the Hall of Fame. They formed a great bond that lasted until Rizzuto's death in 2007 at age 89.

Phil was put in an assisted living facility when he became ill toward the end of his life. It was about 30 minutes away from where Yogi lived and every single day Yogi would drive there to play cards with him. When Phil would start to fall asleep Yogi held his hand and wouldn't leave until Phil would go to sleep. That's what teammates meant to Yogi Berra.

When they were on this trip to Vienna Yogi looked out for Phil as they visited the various locations, like helping him up staircases.

CHOIRBOYS AND YANKEES

The following day Yogi, Whitey, Phil, and their group visited Augarten Palace, which has served as a boarding school for the Vienna Boys Choir since 1948. They climbed the staircase to an auditorium used for private concerts given to dignitaries and iconic Hall of Fame baseball players.

Yogi and his wife Carmen sat in the audience waiting to hear these famous and talented young boys sing. Yogi was known to say, "Always go to other people's funerals, otherwise they won't come to yours.

"Yogi, you are from St. Louis, we live in New Jersey, and you played ball in New York. If you go before I do, where would you like me to have you buried?" Carmen once asked.

"Surprise me," Yogi said.

Yogi Berra's Last Game

When the concert ended the Hall of Fame Yankees legends began to autograph the baseball bat they brought to the choirboys.

"No kidding... they play baseball!" Phil exclaimed as he autographed the bat all the players would sign for the choirboys. "I thought you played soccer?"

"We do," a choirboy replied.

"You play soccer too." Phil said. Whitey stood beside Phil waiting for his turn to autograph the bat.

Yogi burst out laughing, as I squeezed past him through the crowd.

"Whitey's leading guys,"Ralph Branca joked. Whitey sat at the piano and brandished an autographed baseball bat, like a conductor's baton. Choirboys, along with everyone, smiled and laughed as they watched him from behind the piano.

"Did you get the picture yet?" Whitey asked as he sat at the piano. Yogi and Phil laughed at their old teammate known as the "Chairman of the Board".

"He got it Whitey, leading them," Ralph replied. Whitey conducted with the autographed Louisville Slugger and hummed his own version of Johann Straus II, The Blue Danube Waltz to the crowd. "Do, do, do, do, do... do, do... do, do," Whitey hummed. The bat swayed back and forth in his hand like a conductor's baton.

Whitey was born on Sunday, October 21, 1928, in New York, New York. He was 21 years old when he broke into the big leagues on July 1, 1950, with the New York Yankees.

Yogi Berra's Last Game

He stood up from the piano and burst out laughing with the befuddled choirboys laughing at his antics.

"Thanks fellas," Whitey said as he turned around and waved to the children in their sailor uniforms. He stood up next to a choirboy with his hand gently on his shoulder and posed for another photo.

Yogi Berra's Last Game

"Good," Whitey said with a nod of appreciation. He had really broken the ice and set the mood, of that September afternoon, for everyone.

"He's the oldest... he's thirteen," Ralph Branca told Whitey, as he pointed to the boy nearest him. "Thirteen years old?" Ralph asked the choirboy.

"Fourteen," replied the choirboy.

"Fourteen," Ralph replied. "No brothers... no brothers here?"

"No," replied the choirboy.

The Vienna Boys Choir lined up and posed with the Phil "Scooter" Rizzuto "Holy Cow" 1994 Hall of Fame inductee tee shirts they received.

A short time later the players and wives were given a private tour of Palais Augarten, while the choirboys changed into their tee shirts so they could play ball. Yogi and Bill strolled through the tour and talked while they waited for the boys..

Whitey walked past me with Ralph and Mrs. Branca as they explored

Yogi Berra's Last Game

the décor of the elegant rooms the choirboys lived in. It sure ain't The Hill in St. Louis, Missouri where Yogi grew up as a child of Italian immigrants or Astoria, Mount Vernon or Brooklyn, NY where Whitey, Ralph and Phil grew up as kids during and after the Great Depression. Ralph stopped in front of me to spread his long, three-time All-Star pitching arms.

"And now for my last number," Ralph joked, as though he'd follow the choirboys with his own performance.

Whitey stopped to look at a stuffed lion on the bed of a choirboy in one of several bedrooms the boys occupy.

"Isn't that adorable?" a lady asked Whitey.

"Yeah," Whitey replied.

"Isn't that cute?" the lady asked.

"Yeah," Whitey replied.

Whitey walked towards Cora Rizzuto who stood in the doorway of another bedroom. She pointed to a cross of Jesus that hung on the wall.

Yogi Berra's Last Game

They left the bedroom entrance and followed everybody outside onto the soccer field. The choirboys had transformed into children playing like their own children back home in America.

Phil walked across the field and approached a choirboy in front of the soccer net.

"Let me borrow your glove?" Phil asked. The boy politely handed his glove to Phil. "You were with the boys that were singing," Phil said.

"Yes," the boy replied.

"You are terrific... I want to tell yah!" Phil exclaimed.

Phil put his suit jacket next to the soccer net and jogged to the outfield for a hit to come his way. It wasn't long before a choirboy hit a line drive across the soccer field to Phil, who caught it in his glove. Biil White stood in the background watching his old broadcast buddy.

"Yeah!" the crowd of onlookers, ball players and choirboys cheered.

"I got a shortstop!" someone in the crowd shouted, referring to Phil's playing position as a Yankees. Phil threw the ball to the pitcher and ran back to the outfield, like a happy-go-lucky kid from Brooklyn.

When Bill White started play-by-play with Phil to broadcast his first spring-training game, the "Scooter" saw Joe DiMaggio in the stands. Phil ran out of the booth to greet his old teammate and left White on his own. Bill White survived and started a rewarding partnership with Phil Rizzuto.

Yogi Berra's Last Game

Yogi tried to understand what the Austrian choirboys were saying as he smiled and signed autographs for them. Fifty years before, Yogi was a nineteen year old teenager serving in the Navy during World War II, defending children against Hitler and the Nazis. Those children could have been the grandparents of these autograph seeking choirboys.

Phil stood out on the field waiting for the exhilaration of a baseball to come his way. Choirboys approached him for his autograph.

"That's my shirt you're wearing. That's the way I looked when I was young," Phil said as he autographed the back of the tee shirt the choirboy wore, which was adorned by his slightly younger face. "What's your name?" Phil asked.

"Ludwig," the choirboy replied.

"Ludwig! Oh... you're going after the big guys... huh!" Phil teased. The choirboy didn't seem to understand Phil's Ludwig van Beethoven joke. "How old are you?" Phil asked

"Eleven," the choirboy answered. Phil finished with the autograph and got back into playing position.

"These guys gettin in front of me," Phil said about the guys hogging his spot. He suddenly turned to me while keeping an eye on the pitcher.

Yogi Berra's Last Game

"Did you get that catch I made on short up? You got it?" Phil asked while I filmed him.

"Yeah," I replied. He quickly turned away when he heard the crack of a ball that might be hit to him.

There was a commotion in the air when Yogi walked past the soccer goal in his suit, tie and a baseball bat to home plate. Stacked schoolbooks made up the home plate he stood beside as he gripped the bat and took a few warm up swings.

"Throw it underhand!" Phil shouted before the first pitch was thrown.

Choirboys surrounded Yogi while they watched him take warm up swings. How could they possibly know they were watching an iconic baseball player, who in the 1950 season struck out only 12 times in 597 times at bat. A player who holds World Series records by a catcher for most times at bat, most hits, and most doubles. He is third for the most homeruns scored in World Series play. Mickey Mantle has 18, Babe Ruth has 15 and Yogi Berra has 12. During a nineteen-year playing career he hit over .300 in four seasons, had more than twenty home runs eleven times, and had five 100-plus runs-batted-in (RBI) seasons. His best season at the plate was 1956, when he hit .298, had thirty home runs, and batted in 105 runs.

How could they possibly know they were watching an iconic baseball player who in the 1950 season struck out only 12 times in 597 times at bat.

"If I can see it, I can hit it," Yogi once said.

The pitch was thrown by Dell. Yogi swung and missed.

"Ohhh!" the crowd groaned. The next pitch was thrown and Yogi hit a pop fly down the field.

Yogi Berra's Last Game

"Yeah!" the crowd cheered. Two choirboys sprinted as fast as they could after the ball.

Yogi waited for another pitch when Bill White shouted at him from the outfield.

"Two swings, you're out!" Bill shouted. Yogi burst out laughing at Bill's comment, while he comfortably held the bat. The pitch was thrown and Yogi timed his swing as he watched the ball float through the air.

Yogi Berra stood in the lefthand batter's box at Yankee Stadium for his first major league game. Twenty-seven months before he was in the D-Day invasion. Connie Mack's Philadelphia Athletic's pitcher Jesse Flores threw an outside curveball and Yogi cracked his first homerun into the rightfield seats. The following day, he smacked another one. He entered the game when it was all-white and left when indoor baseball arrived as the unchallenged American pastime. Nobody except Stan Musial drove in more runs than the beloved Yogi Berra from 1947 - 1961.

Yogi Berra's Last Game

"Oh, oh, oh!" Bill and Phil exclaimed, as the ball flew through the air. Yogi slammed a pop fly to right field for the first time in years. He could still hit.

Yogi Berra's Last Game

A choirboy sprinted for the ball and caught it. Yogi was out.

"All right!" Phil and Bill cheered along with the crowd. Yogi walked past the soccer goal with the bat over his shoulder and handed it to the next choirboy who came to bat. The next pitch was thrown to the choirboy and he hit a pop fly.

"Oh, oh Whitey!" Bill exclaimed.

The opportunity to bat after Yogi Berra hits, at this point in his legendary career, would be a once in a lifetime exeperience for anyone. Maybe a little bit of the Yogi magic rubbed onto the bat.

Whitey stood in the outfield and stretched his arm over his head to catch the pop fly that was just out of his reach. A choirboy raced past him to grab the ball off the ground. Whitey looked into his hand and comically pretended to see if the ball was there.

A short while later a choirboy hit a pop fly to left field as Yogi was walking on the side of the soccer field.

"Heads up!" Heads up!" the crowd shouted. Yogi covered his head and the ball just missed him.

Phil waited with glove ready as the next choirboy hit a pop fly. He ran up and caught it. Phil looked up the field to throw the ball to a choirboy.

"Here yah are tiger! Hey Johan!" Phil jolkingly shouted, as he threw the ball to the choirboy.

The choirboys continued to take their turns at bat and continued to hit the ball. Maybe it was some kind of osmosis, an unconscious absorption of knowledge through continual exposure that was rubbing off when they watched Yogi hit. Whatever it was, the boys were hitting and Phil kept playing. Another choirboy came up to bat and hit a pop fly to the outfield.

"I got it... it's right there White!" Phil shouted. "I'll get it!" The seventy-seven year old Scooter ran past Bill like a kid to get the ball.

"You feel that good?" Bill shouted.

"Yeah!" Phil shouted back, as he ran across the field to get the ball.

"Jesus!" Bill shouted. "You feel pretty good!" Bill laughed as Phil picked up the ball and threw it to a choirboy. He punched the pocket of his glove and ran back to his position before the next pitch.

"Alright let's go... this is my play!" Phil exclaimed. "Little double play right here!"

Yogi Berra's Last Game

I walked over to where Yogi and Bill stood beside each other assessing the batting skills of a choirboy, as though they were on a scouting mission for the Yankees.

"He's got a pretty good swing," Yogi remarked.

"Hey... let that big kid hit!" Bill shouted to the pitcher. "He hit that ball way down there!"

"The kid's hitting cross hand," Yogi said.

"Who?" Bill asked.

"The kid here... the guy just up there," Yogi replied. "He's hit that cross hand."

"Oh yeah... yeah, yeah!" Bill replied. "Here he is... right here." The boy slammed a linedrive to the outfield.

"Ha, ha," Yogi chuckled.

"We got another Henry Aaron!" Bill exclaimed.

"You give 100 percent in the first half of the game, and if that isn't enough, in the second half you give what's left," Yogi once said.

Another choirboy came up to bat and hit a grounder that went between the legs of two other choirboys.

Yogi Berra's Last Game

Fortunately there was a catcher who backed them up. Yogi snagged the ball and tossed it back to the choirboy.

A shortime later Phil and a choirboy in the outfield went to catch a pop fly. The choirboy made a great catch.

"Nice play!' Phil exclaimed. The choirboy threw the ball back to the pitcher. "Give me five!" Phil exclaimed as he extended his palm.

The choirboy slapped the palm of his hand and Phil jumped back. "Oh!" Phil moaned with an insincere grimace. He walked a few feet away and turned around to the boys. "Boy... he almost broke my hand!" Phil teased. The confused choirboys didn't know whether to laugh or run from a spanking as a man their grandfather's age kidded around with them.

Yogi Berra's Last Game

Yogi diligently autographed the back of a choirboy's tee shirt as he laughed at Phil's antics.

"I haven't played a guy right yet!" Phil exclaimed. A moment later Phil noticed several choirboys standing in line behind him getting autographs from Yogi and endearingly nudged one with his glove.

"Boys… on the bench!" a man yelled as he pointed across the field. A herd of choirboys stampeded across the field to where Whitey Ford sat on a bench under a tree in the shade talking with Bill White. All of a sudden they were mobbed by autograph seeking choirboys.

Whitey began to autograph the tee shirts of choirboys while Bill could be heard in the background.

"I got you… I got you… I got you… I didn't get you." Bill said as he found the backs of a choirboy without his autograph.

At 5'10" tall, Whitey Ford is one of three pitchers in the Hall of Fame born since 1900 who were under six fee tall. He was named the World Series Most Valuable Player in 1961.

Yogi Berra's Last Game

Whitey stood on the bench to see over the heads of the choirboys as he searched for shirts he hadn't autographed.

"We're trying to teach them!" Whitey shouted to Yogi and Phil. "We want to sing to them... Take Me Out To The Ballgame!"

"Do you know Take Me Out To The Ballgame?" Phil asked the choirboys who surrounded him.

"No," the choirboys said shaking their heads.

"No!" Phil exclaimed. He stood with a choirboy's glove on his hand. "I gave them everything they need to know," Phil said. "How to be a winning player."

"That's nice but they can't understand yah," Bill teased as he sat on the bench and continued autographing the backs of choirboy tee shirts.

"Little League baseball is a very good thing because it keeps the parents off the streets," Yogi once said.

Yogi Berra's Last Game

"I think Little League is wonderful. It keeps the kids out of the house," Yogi once said.

Phil raised the baseball glove he borrowed from a choirboy, over his head. "Hey! Whose glove is this?" Phil shouted to the crowd of choirboys surrounding him. "Whose glove is this?" A choirboy walked up and Phil gave him his glove. "Thank you very much!" Phil exclaimed.

A moment later Whitey walked through the crowd of choirboys, around the bench and raised his arms like a maestro. Yogi, Phil and Enos walked over and stood beside him to sing the Yankees version of "Take Me Out To The Ballgame" to the Vienna choirboys. The song was quickly re-written as they sung the home team lyrics of the song.

"Root... root, root for the Yankees!" the four Hall of Fame players sang in harmony.

Yogi Berra's Last Game

Yogi put his arms around the shoulders of Enos and Whitey as they sang. The camaraderie of the teammates, they were and still are, could be felt as they finished singing the song. You probably never forget winning a World Series together. Yogi's pinky finger was adorned with a ring.

"Wait a minute... wait a minute! We didn't even get a hand here!" Phil exclaimed, as a second rendition of the song was about to begin. "They didn't even applaud." The crowd laughed as the Hall of Fame Legends and choirboys began to sing together this time. The crowd cheered when the Yankees and choirboys finished their version of an American classic.

"It ain't over 'til it's over" made Yogi, as The New Yorker wrote in 1991, the successor to Churchill as the most quotable figure in the world.

The group disbanded and Yogi continued signing autographs to make sure he each choirboy had his name on their new tee shirt's.

"Yeah... you got me already," Yogi told a choirboy who didn't know he had his autograph.

Yogi Berra's Last Game

Yogi searched the backs of choirboy's to find a tee shirt he hadn't signed. "I ain't got him yet... turn around." Yogi ordered. The choirboy squirmed about as Yogi autographed the back of his tee shirt in the crowd. Yogi, Whitey and Phil's autographs could be seen on every kid.

"Okay," Yogi told the choirboy as he finished. Once again as Yogi has said, "It ain't over till it's over."

"Don't move... don't move," Phil said as he carefully autographed the back of a squirming choirboy's tee shirt. "Don't breathe."

Phil looked around for choirboys who didn't have his autograph. "Did I get everybody?" Phil asked as he noticed a choirboy's back without his name. "Oh... I didn't get this guy with the big shoulders... Holy Cow!" Phil exclaimed as he signed the boy's tee shirt. "Would you think that the picture you have on your chest is me?"

"I know it was," the choirboy replied. "You don't look like it."

"But I don't look like it," Phil replied. "I know it... that was a long time ago."

"It says holy cow," the choirboy remarked.

"Holy cow!" Phil exclaimed as he chuckled. "You got to practice a

Yogi Berra's Last Game

song and end it with holy cow." Phil diligently autographed the tee shirts of the seemingly never-ending line of choirboys. He finally caught up to the autographs of Yogi, Whitey and Bill as the picture of the tee shirts reveal. "Look it… these kids are really something," Phil remarked. "They're lined up very neatly.

Phil Rizzuto was born on Tuesday, September 25, 1917, in Brooklyn, New York and died Monday, August 14, 2007 at 89 years old. He was twenty-three years old when he broke into the big leagues on April 14, 1941. Phil was a diminutive five feet, six inches tall, but there wasn't a better shortstop in his era. He was Casey Stengel's "little fella." Phil was an All-Star five times in the American League. He called Yankees games for WPIX-TV, Channel 11 as a broadcaster until 1996.

Seventy-eight year old Enos "Country" Slaughter sat under the tree on the bench, autographing the choirboy's tee shirts along with the seventy-seven year old "Scooter." "Did I get everybody?" Phil looked about for a tee shirt without his name on it.

Yogi and Whitey stood amongst the crowd of people watching the choirboys after they finished their autographing duties.

"The shirt almost touches the ground on the little one," a guy from the crowd said. "They had to pin it up in his pants." Yogi clapped his hands and laughed along with Whitey, who stood nonchalantly behind him, with his suit jacket over his shoulder.

"Mr. Berra," Casey Stengel said in the Sporting News in 1949, "is a very strange fellow of very remarkable abilities."

Yogi Berra's Last Game

"This one here?" Yogi asked as he pointed at the boy.

"The little one," Whitey said.

"Phil don't even fit in there," Yogi teased. "It's too big for Phil!" Yogi noticed the shoes of Mrs. Ford as he stood with Whitey. "I told Cora... they get a new pair and they go out and buy some more Whitey." Whitey and Mrs. Ford laughed. "A nickel ain't worth a dime anymore," Yogi once said.

Joan Foran lived across the street from Edward Charles "Whitey" Ford on 34th Avenue in Astoria, Queens and married him on April 14, 1951 in St. Patrick's Church in Long Island City.

The afternoon slipped away as Phil continued playing with the kids and coached them on their baseball skills.

"Nice play," Phil said as he caught the ball and threw it back to the choirboy. "I said throw a grounder... he's throwing these bullets to me! The choirboy threw another ball to Phil. "Not that hard!" Phil exclaimed as he caught the ball. "Make them bounce out here!" Phil pointed to a spot on the field.

He threw the ball back to the choirboy. "Okay!" Phil exclaimed. The choirboy caught it and threw the ball back to Phil.

"That's it!" Phil exclaimed as he caught it. "Little double play!" He threw the ball back to the choirboy.

"Do you play ping pong?" the boy asked Phil. He caught the ball and

Yogi Berra's Last Game

threw it back to the boy.

"What?' Phil asked.

"Do you play ping pong?' the choirboy asked again. Phil caught the grounder thrown by the choirboy.

"Ping pong!" Phil exclaimed. "I'm a great ping pong player!"

"Where's the bat?" Phil asked. A choirboy ran up and handed him a bat. Phil, who was regarded as one of the greatest bunters in the history of baseball, got into his bunting stance to teach the choirboys. "Come on!" Phil shouted as he gripped the bat.

The choirboys ran to the outfield because they thought he was hitting balls to them. "No, no, no!" Phil shouted. "Bunt!" He waved the boys back, as he held the bat. "Come here... I want to show you the correct way to bunt… like this," Phil instructed. "Come on."

Yogi Berra's Last Game

The choirboy retrieved the ball and tossed it to another choirboy. "You huckleberries!" Phil shouted as the boy walked up to take the bat from him. "No... wait... let me..." Phil began to say as he laughed. "Come on... one more bunt!" Phil took a warm up swing. "Watch it... one more bunt!" Phil exclaimed. "Come on... let's go!" The choirboy pitched the ball to him but he missed the bunt expressing an embarrassed grimace. "Ohhh," the crowd groaned. A 5-foot-6-inch leadoff man, Rizzuto was a superb bunter, used to good advantage by NY Yankees teams that won 11 pennants and played in a total of nine World Series between while Phil played with them between 1941 and 1956. Rizzuto tried out with the Brooklyn Dodgers and New York Giants when he was 16, but because of his size, Dodgers manager Casey Stengel, told him to "Go get a shoeshine box." He went on to become one of Stengel's most dependable players with the Yanks.

Phil went back to his bunting position. "This is the bean out bunt!"
Phil shouted to the boys. The choirboy pitched the ball .

Yogi Berra's Last Game

"There it is!" Phil exclaimed as he bunted the ball and took off like he was running to first base.

Phil ran around choirboys like they were slalom poles.

He leaped into the air between them.

Yogi Berra's Last Game

"Safe!" Phil exclaimed as he landed on his feet.

He looked at the choirboys surrounding him, who wore his face on their oversized autographed tee shirts. "Go ahead," Phil said. "You hit now."

The afternoon with the choirboys was coming to an end so Phil checked the backs of their tee shirts to make sure he didn't miss signing any autographs. "You got Phil Rizzuto… that's me," he said. "I signed that… I signed that."

Phil stood looking about for a moment and turned to me. "These kids are great, aren't they," Phil remarked. "Unbelievable!"

Yogi Berra's Last Game

"Home head the weary warriors," Ralph Branca joked as he walked by me toward the bus. "If we ever play a game we'll never make it."

Yogi and Whitey headed back to the bus. Their visit with the Vienna Boys Choir had come to an end.

"It's tough to make predictions, especially when it involves the future," Yogi once said. Einstein and Mark Twain also said a version, but Yogi didn't know it. It was an original thought for Yogi like every "Yogi-ism".

"So long kids," Phil said as he walked past me to the bus. I hurried back to the bus as Phil and Cora were having a comical argument. She had taken her shoes off and walked in the grass with bare feet while she waited for him.

"You... I swear... if I tell her not to do something!" Phil exclaimed.

Cora stepped onto the bus entrance but suddenly turned around and stomped on the grass again in her bare feet. "Get out of there... God damn it!" Phil shouted. "I'm gonna... you never saw me mad... did yah?" Cora walked towards him with a threatening smile on her face. "I'm not gonna get mad either!" Phil exclaimed as he scooted out of reach towards the bus. "That's alright... just want..." Phil began to say as he followed Cora to the bus steps. "Come on... we're going in the wrong way Cora."

"Not me!" Cora exclaimed. "I'm going in the right way!"

"I'll never last," Phil said exhaustedly, as he followed his wife into the bus. "I'll never last."

Phil married Cora Anne Ellenborn on June 23, 1943. They met the previous year when Phil substituted for Joe DiMaggio as a speaker at Newwark communion breakfast. Cora was born February 17, 1920 and passed away on October 7, 2010. She lived three years after Phil's death on August 13, 2007. She was 90 years old.

Yogi Berra's Last Game

Schonbrunn Palace

Yogi and Enos walked towards the entrance of the Schonbrunn Palace in Vienna.

"Where'd they play Army at?" Yogi asked.

"At Duke last night," Enos replied. "I tried to get a score but I haven't gotten one."

"Thursday night they played them?" Yogi asked.

"Yeah." Enos replied. "It was on ESPN last night."

"That's the one they do every Thursday," Yogi said.

"Yeah," Enos replied. "Where's the, ah? All our group together now?"

"Yeah," Yogi replied as he walked quickly to catch up with Phil and Cora.

Yogi was an All-Star for fifteen years in the MLB. He received MVP votes in fifteen consecutive season and is second in number of votes for MVP behind Hank Aaron who had nineteen votes. He is one of six managers who took teams from both the American League and National League to the World Series. Yogi died September 22, 2015 at the age of ninety. His incredible life and accomplishments live on through The Yogi Berra Museum and Learning Center in Little Falls, New Jersey.

The weather was overcast and umbrellas opened as it began to drizzle. Mrs. Berra stood with Mrs. Ford sharing her umbrella until Bill White's daughter handed Mrs. Berra an umbrella.

"For you ma'am," she said.

"Thank you," Mrs. Berra said graciously. Carmen, Cora, Phil and Yogi stood and viewed the palace park like tourists. Cora began taking pictures while Phil held the umbrella.

Yogi Berra's Last Game

Bill White's six foot three inch frame unintentionally stood in front of the diminutive five foot six inch Scooter and his wife.

"White... get out of the way!" Phil shouted comically.

I walked towards Cora and Phil as she took pictures with her instamatic camera. Yogi walked between Cora's view and my lens, which clearly added to her frustration.

"Look at this," Phil said as he stood holding the umbrella.

"He's gonna eyeball us with that camera!" Cora exclaimed as she looked up at me from her camera.

Phil began laughing hysterically as Cora walked away to take another angle of the picture.

Yogi inadvertently walked away with the umbrella that was loaned to his wife Carmen. Bill White's daughter who loaned it walked up behind Yogi.

"Mr. Berra!" she teased.

"What do yah want?" Yogi asked as he turned around.

She reached for the umbrella. "I gave this umbrella to your wife," she replied.

"Okay," Yogi replied as he handed her the umbrella without hesitation.

"I wish I had an answer to that, because I'm tired of answering that question," Yogi once said.

"You may share with her," she teased. "But you may not take it from her." A grin of embarrassement began to grow on Yogi's face.

"I don't like the rain," Yogi replied. He laughed and zipped his jacket. She handed the umbrella back to Carmen.

"It ain't the heat, it's the humility," Yogi once said.

Phil and Cora stood waiting for Carmen to take their picture. Yogi once again held the umbrella as Carmen got her Kodak disposable camera ready. Yogi pointed at Phil and Cora directing the shot for his wife. "Phil! Phil!" Yogi shouted. "Phil!"

A guy named Bobby, who was assisting the tour, stood too close to Phil and Cora as Yogi directed the shot. "Hey… ah… Bobby! Get out of the way!" Yogi shouted impatiently. "Phil! Turn around!" Carmen was nearly ready to take Phil and Cora's picture. "Hold it!" Yogi shouted, as he held up his hand in a halting motion. "Hold it! Phil, hold it!"

"Get back!" Carmen shouted.

Yogi Berra's Last Game

Yogi grinned at Phil and Cora as Carmen took the picture.

"Okay," Yogi said as he grinned his funny and endearing grin.

"Let's go take a walk," Phil said to Cora. They began to stroll through the palace park taking pictures. "This is unbelievable. It's got to be at least a mile wide," Phil said as he held the umbrella over Cora. "Wait. Do you want to get up closer?" Phil asked.

"No… It's too cold," Cora replied.

Yogi Berra's Last Game

They began walking back to the palace when the tip of a rib of the umbrella poked Phil on the side of his head causing him to flinch. "He's so afraid a little umbrellas gonna touch him," Cora teased. "He's gonna have a heart attack." On their walk back Phil was told to get back to the tour group because they were going inside the palace.

"Cora! They want us quickly!" Phil exclaimed "On the double!" He began to walk backward quickly.

"See the lighting," someone said.

"Where?" Phil asked. "You got be kidding! No kidding?" Phil continued walking backwards. "Oh, oh. Lightning!" Phil exclaimed as he saw it strike. He started jogging backwards. "Let's go!" Phil exclaimed. He picked up his pace for several strides and spun off one foot into a pirouette, which nearly caused him to fall down.

"Showoff!" Cora scolded.

"I'm not a showoff!" Phil exclaimed.

"You are!" Cora scolded.

"If I was a showoff!" Phil exclaimed. "I was gonna hurdle over that Japanese lady there!"

A short time later on our way back to the palace Phil commented to me.

"You really gonna be in shape!" Phil exclaimed. "I'll tell yah that!"

"He works very, very hard!" Cora exclaimed. "Really he has!"

"I think the kid deserves a hand!" Phil exclaimed as he clapped his hands.

Phil was a popular and beloved broadcaster for Yankees fans who punctuated his game-calling with birthday wishes to them.

The tour group was listening to the guide when Phil and Cora caught up to them inside the palace.

"Hey! Rizzuto!" Bill White scolded jokingly. "Will you stay with the group?"

The palace tour continued with the guide giving them a special tour of art that was off limits to the general public and photographs.

Carmen and Yogi listened quietly to the tour guide.

"This is not part of the normal tour and not many of the guides can do this part. I thought it would be a bit of a treat. It's not available to the public," the Tour Guide said.

Yogi Berra's Last Game

The tour went through the Great Gallery of the palace where official ceremonies and activities have been held throughout history.

Carmen and Yogi seemed captivated by the art and tour guide's spiel. He told them stories and facts about rulers like Napoleon who had lived in the palace.

I was bashful, nervous, not good looking. I could hardly believe my luck," said Yogi when he first met his wife. "Carmen liked me as much as I liked her."

Yogi Berra's Last Game

"This is unbelievable. I'll tell yah that," Phil remarked as he observed the ceilings. "The Italians would paint upside down." As the tour continued and the guide's spiel became tedious to Phil, he needed to shake things up. "I'm dying to make a face right in the camera," Phil said to me.

"Be my guest," I replied.

"Hang in there Phil," Enos urged.

Phil waited for the moment he thought Cora wouldn't see him and then made a funny face into the camera.

"I don't know... the cameras driving me nuts!" Phil exclaimed. "Don't tell Cora I did that."

Phil recalled when he first met Cora in 1943. "I fell in love so hard I didn't go home." He rented a hotel room nearby for for a month to be near her while he was playing for the Yankees. They had three daughters Cindy, Patricia, Penny and son Phil.

Phil continued on with the tour and behaved as well as he could. "Where's Cora?" Phil asked looking about. "Cora's in back." Phil continued to walk along as he watched for Cora. "I'm not gonna make that... Cora's in the back." he said cautiously. "I'm not gonna make that face." Cora appeared from the crowd and walked towards Phil. "Don't you... listen he's... Cora it's not my fault," Phil said timidly. "It's his fault."

Yogi Berra's Last Game

Cora walked by and Phil quickly made another funny face.

They continued on with the palace tour but it didn't deter Phil from his tomfoolery. Tony Veteri, a former NFL Super Bowl referee, was on the trip and gave Phil some referee lessons. "Okay... Holding. Number twenty-seven. Fifteen yards. First down," Phil said.

"Excellent!" Tony remarked. "Excellent!"

"Pretty good referee... right," Phil said. He joked around with me as I filmed him strolling through the crowd in the palace. "You're doing a terrific job. This is the hardest job in here. We only got about two hundred rooms to go... so you can make it," Phil teased.

The palace tour went past a famous painting of illusion, which interested Yogi.

"Isn't that something? Oh, no kidding! It's so interesting," Phil said. "I got to brush up on it. Make sure you get a shot of this guy. His eyes follow you all over the room as you're walking. I think it's Franz Joseph. He had big feet!"

Carmen went to the gift shop at the end of the Schonbrunn Palace tour and Yogi decided to wait outside.

"I let her go," Yogi told Bill. "I don't want to shop… she's fine."

Carmen Short was born in Salem, Missouri on September 24, 1928 and married Yogi Berra on January 16, 1949. They met when she was a waitress at Biggie's steakhouse restaurant in St. Louis after he returned from World War II. Yogi courted her on the road during his baseball career with the Yankees. He wrote, "I do miss you always. I am always thinking about you." He proposed to Carmen at dinner in his family's home and they were married for 65 years. "Yogi said it best," Carmen would say. "We have a good time together even when we're not together." Carmen passed away on Thursday, March 6, 2014 at the age of 85.

Yogi Berra's Last Game

Yogi strolled across the courtyard with Bill and Enos back to the bus.

"Pretty good walk to walk, all the way around this thing," Enos remarked.

Phil and Cora saw me on their way back from the palace to the bus.
"Hey!" Phil shouted.

Yogi Berra's Last Game

"Give me your personal feelings?" I asked.

"How is everything in America?" Phil asked. "Season still on? The Strike over?" He shook his head with a grimace. "Can't believe it!"

"I tell yah... this is very, very beautiful but I'm very happy I didn't live in this era. You got to be real tough. I mean... you'd freeze in the winter and you just drown in your own perspiration in the summer. You had to wear shoes with big heels on them," Phil joked. "It is beautiful though."

"Where are we going now?" I asked.

"We're going... ha, ha," Phil chuckled. "Back on the bus to another castle! I can't believe it!"

"Did Yogi give you any feelings on the palace?" I asked. Phil laughed as he inserted a mint into his mouth.

"Yeah, Yogi said... how'd you like to have to pay for heat in this place in the winter? Old Yogi," Phil said fondly.

He walked backward waving good-bye, with one hand then the other. "We don't want to miss the bus!" Phil shouted. "I'm fading away."

Yogi Berra's Last Game

I walked up to Yogi at the front gate of the palace.

"Phil said you were saying it was hard to heat that place," I told Yogi.

"Heat it!" Yogi exclaimed with a grin. "They got good heat in there."

I went to see Phil, while Yogi stood at the front gate of the Schonbrunn Palace waiting patiently for Mrs. Berra to come back from the gift shop. Yogi has said, "You can observe a lot by just watching."

Yogi Berra's Last Game

Phil stood on the sidewalk next to the refreshment cart and held an ice cream cone.

"How much is the ice cream?" Phil asked. "I just want to see how much it is."

"I guess you need to fill up on those calories after that hike," I said to Phil.

"Oh... and we got another one to go!" Phil exclaimed with a grimace.

"We're getting the right change," Phil said. "You want something?"

"Yeah, I'll have an ice cream," I replied. The "Scooter" bought me an ice cream cone.

"You better cut the pizza in four pieces because I'm not hungry enough to eat six," Yogi once said to an employee at a pizzeria.

He stood with a cone in one hand and pointed down the sidewalk with the other. "Did you see me get weighed over there?" Phil asked.

"Weighed?" I asked.

"On that machine," Phil replied, as he pointed down the sidewalk at a scale. "And Ted got on it and it went all the way around twice!" Ted was a gentleman, of large proportion, on the group tour.

Yogi Berra's Last Game

Phil walked down the sidewalk toward the street scale. He put a coin in it and watched the needle go around and stop.

"How much do you weigh?" I asked. I held the ice cream cone Phil bought me in one hand and my camera in the other. Phil looked closely at the needle on the scale.

"Sixty-seven!" he exclaimed as he stepped off the scale onto the sidewalk. "What is sixty-seven?" He took a bite of his ice cream cone and stared at me as though I knew how to convert kilos into pounds.

"What is sixty-seven?" Phil asked again.

Yogi Berra's Last Game

"Sixty-seven," Phil said. "What do you do?" He took another bite of his cone.

He realized an answer wasn't coming so he turned around and walked to the bus.

"I don't know how to multiply that," I replied.

What's sixty-seven?" Phil asked.

In kilos, it was, and still is 147.4 pounds.

Chapter 5

Castle Kreuzenstein

It wasn't June 16, 1944 when nineteen year old Yogi Berra fought on Omaha Beach during the D-Day invasion of Normandy. But fifty years later at sixty-nine he could climb a hill pretty well.

Crunch, crunch could be heard under foot as I followed Yogi up the steep gravel road through the forest to Castle Kreuzenstein.

"You gonna sleep good," Yogi said to Cora.

The tower of the Castle appeared through the trees as they reached the top of the road. It was a peculiar sight to see Phil, Yogi, Whitey and their wives hiking towards a castle through a forest.

"Dracula's up there," Phil said as they approached the castle. "It looks scary up there."

Yogi strolled across the bridge, which spanned a moat, to the castle entrance.

"How old is this castle?" Yogi asked.

"About three hundred years," the tour guide replied.

Yogi Berra's Last Game

Phil, Enos, Yogi and Bill walked through the ancient courtyard of Castle Kreuzenstein, which has been used as a location for films. The Three Musketeers was filmed here in1993. Phil zipped his jacket when the cold Austrian wind blew through the castle walls as it had for centuries.

Joan Ford and Cora Rizzuto quickly hiked the steep alley trying to stay warm inside the old castle walls.

"Are we in the Alps?" Joan exclaimed as she laughed.

"How are you?" I asked politely.

"We're cold right now!" Joan exclaimed.

"We're hungry!" Cora exclaimed. She pulled the collar up on her jacket. They both laughed and walked quickly past me up the steep hill.

Yogi Berra's Last Game

Phil nearly twisted his ankle trying to keep up with his wife and Joan.

"Cora!" Phil shouted

"Your wife is kicking your butt up the hill," I teased.

"I know it!" Phil exclaimed as he walked past me laughing. "Those women have got some stamina."

He picked up a pebble and tossed it at Cora like a newly inducted 1994 Hall of Fame shortstop. Phil's number 10 was retired by the New York Yankees in 1985.

"What a life!" Enos exclaimed as he hiked slowly past me smiling. Enos was born April 27, 1916 and passed away August 12, 2002 at the age of 86 years old.

Carmen followed Yogi up the hill and attempted to take his picture. "Slow down Yogi!" Carmen shouted. "Yogi!" He turned around and she snapped the picture. Carmen Berra grew up one of six children in Salem, Mo., two hours from The Hill — Yogi's boyhood Italian immigrant neighborhood in St. Louis. Yogi continued exploring the Castle walls.

"What do you think?" I asked.

"What do I think?" Yogi replied repeating my question. "I don't know yet... I haven't been inside."

Yogi talked to the tour guide while they waited for the big iron door of the castle to open.

Yogi Berra's Last Game

"Open says of me!" Dell Alston chanted as he walked up. "Open says of me!"

Bill White leaned against the railing of the bridge with a grin on his face as he watched. Dell walked so close to the iron door his nose nearly touched. He abruptly stopped and looked over at Phil. "Doesn't work Phil! Wait, wait, wait!" Del exclaimed as he began chanting Phil's infamous phrase. "Holy cow! Holy cow! That doesn't work either. Yo bro! Open the door! That don't work either!" Phil and Cora laughed along with the crowd. One of Phil's most famous calls on WCBS radio saying "Holy Cow" was when he called Roger Maris 61st Home Run on WCBS radio.

The immense iron door of the castle was finally opened. Cora led the way as Phil followed closely behind her.

Throughout the week I wasn't sure if I was welcome trudging around with my camera trying to capture historical moments of Yogi as well as the other Hall of Famers. He's a national heirloom who struck out at the plate only 414 times in his 19 year career. Yogi was a superb game caller behind the plate. Casey Stengel managed Berra for years and credited much of the Yankees' success to his catcher. "He looks cumbersome, but he's quick as a cat," said Stengel.

Yogi took me by surprise as he was about to walk past me. The next thing I knew Yogi Berra's eyes and nose filled my camera lens. He stepped back and a huge grin appeared across his face as he began to

Yogi Berra's Last Game

laugh. People think Yogi is funny and he was certainly trying to be here.

"They say he's funny," said Casey Stengel. "Well, he has a lovely wife and family, a beautiful home, money in the bank, and he plays golf with millionaires. What's funny about that?" Yogi Berra is a cultural icon whose fame transcended the baseball diamond. He had a fortunate family.

"The next thing I knew Yogi Berra's eyes and nose filled my camera lens."

"Oh, Mr. Berra is a very sociable fellow. He acts like home plate is his room," Casey Stengel once said. Yogi followed the others into the castle.

Yogi Berra's Last Game

He entered a room with medieval weaponry including a catapult, cannons, cannon balls lined up on the floor, sleighs and a medieval rack.

"Oh... here we go. Oh... look at that." Yogi enthusiastically observed. "That's the cannon Enos. That's a big cannon."

"That's the cannon... huh," Enos replied. Yogi endeared himself to baseball fans since WWII as a hard working, blue collar man and would always be fascinated with weapons of war no matter what era.

"Hey... hey Yogi!" Joe shouted. "And you say you don't believe in Santa Claus. See... his sleds right here!" Yogi looked at the sleighs hung on the walls.

"I told Phil to lie down," Joe told Whitey. "We'll stretch him on the rack."

Phil walked over and carefully sat down on the wooden slats of the medieval rack for a torturous photo-op.

"You want the rope?" Bob asked as he assisted Phil.

"The rope!" Phil exclaimed. "We got to stretch me!" He leaned back on the rack with his arms outstretched above his head and wrapped the rope around his waste for the picture. "My arms have gotta be down here." Joe walked over to Phil and grabbed Phil's ankles. "No… no… no!" Phil moaned. "Ahhh!"

Yogi Berra's Last Game

Joe stopped and stood up laughing. "Go ahead Joe! Joe...do it again...go ahead," Phil said.

Joe grabbed Phil by the ankles again and pulled his legs to stretch him on the rack.

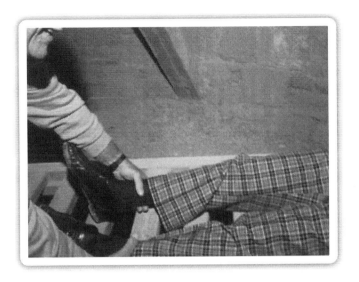

"Ahh! Ohh!" The diminutive Rizzuto groaned. "I'm six foot four!"

Phil started to remove the rope around his waste to get off the rack but stopped when others wanted a picture of him. "Holy cow!" Phil exclaimed. He tried to get his contorted body more comfortable on the wooden rack. Phil wiped the medieval dust from his hands and with a grin, tilted his head back onto the rack for another photo. "Ah!" Phil cried out. "He got me!"

"Wait. Let me get over here," Bob said. "Hold on.

"What?" Phil exclaimed.

"Wait… I gotta get it with your camera," Bob replied.

"Oh, nice going!" Phil exclaimed tortuously. "I go through all that agony."

"The Scooter" played errorless ball in 21 consecutive World Series games as shortstop for the Yankees. Joe DiMaggio said, "the shortstop held the team together."

Yogi Berra's Last Game

Phil leaned back on the rack for another photo as Bob got his camera ready. "Come on!" Phil exclaimed as he lay uncomfortably across the rack. "You got it?" The camera flash went off. "Ahhh!" Phil screamed.

"Phil was a gem, one of the greatest people I ever knew. A dear friend and great teammate," Yogi once said. "When I first came up to the Yankees he was like a big, actually small, brother to me. He's meant an awful lot to baseball, and the Yankees, and has left us with a lot of wonderful memories."

Phil climbed off the rack as quickly as possible and wiped the dust from his clothes. "Did you get a picture of Santa Claus's sleigh?" Phil asked Bob.

"No," Bob replied as he handed Phil the camera. He pointed the camera and took a picture of the sleighs hung on the castle wall.

Phil left the torture chamber and walked towards a stone bench with a cover that looked as if it could be removed like a casket.

"Is that for Dracula?" Phil asked referring to the bench.

"He's in there," Bob replied.

"You want me lying down?" Phil asked, as he sat down on the bench. We laughed at Phil's comment. He thought we wanted another picture with him lying down on the bench like he had on the rack. He threw his arms up in the air and laughed. "I don't know. I'm tired!"

He got off the stone bench laughing. "Dracula's under there," Phil joked. He walked into the courtyard where the group waited and explored the grounds. The outer walls of the castle were peppered with bullet holes from fighting in World War II. During the war Phil served in the Navy and was in charge of a 20mm gun crew on a ship in the Pacific. He contracted malaria serving in New Guinea and was sent to Australia to recover. He coached the US Navy baseball team while he was there.

149

Whitey and Yogi entered a doorway into another room of the castle where there was a stuffed wild boar.

"That's a boar," Bill White told Whitey

"Yeah. I can see," Whitey replied. "Look at the teeth." He examined the wild boar closely and touched it's tusk. "Woo!" He exclaimed.

Yogi Berra's Last Game

Whitey walked into another room and pointed towards the miniature cannons on exhibit. "The Hess… the Hessian army!" Whitey exclaimed. "We're gonna kick their ass!"

Yogi, Whitey, Enos, Bill and Joe stood in a medieval weapons room where suits of armor were exhibited.

"Hey Carmen take a picture," Enos told Mrs. Berra. "What you do is push the button. It's already."

Yogi pointed at a bottle Whitey was holding.

"Don't show that label," Yogi warned Whitey. "Don't show that label." He was the NY Yankees pitcher who won both the Cy Young Award and World Series MVP in 1961. Whitey started eight Game 1's of the World Series and left the game in 1951 and 1952 to serve in the Army during the Korean War. He wasn't worried about showing a beer label even if it was Yogi Berra warning him.

Whitey looked at the label of the bottle he held.

Yogi Berra's Last Game

"Huh... don't show that what?" Bill asked Yogi.

"He can't show that label," Yogi told Bill.

"Oh… it's not his brand," Bill replied.

"Oh yeah!" Whitey scoffed. "Like the other beer company really pays me a lot of money."

"Philip!" Joe shouted as he looked around for "The Scooter.".

"He's on his way back!" someone in the group shouted.

"He's on his way back!" Joe exclaimed. "I wanted to show him his next suit." Whitey began to smile when he heard Joe's comment.

"Over forty years ago we used to work in this shop in Newark... a clothing store... Phil and I... Hermanski and Branca," Whitey recalled.

"What was that called? Where's Yogi?" Whitey pondered the name of the clothing shop and began repeating variations of the name trying to recall it. "The men's shop... Men's shop."

MLB players were fighting over millions they were already earning in 1994, while Whitey was trying to remember the name of the store he and his Hall of Fame teammate worked in the off-season in simpler times. What a difference the abolishment of the reserve clause made, in 1975 and the end of collusion between owners, for players in 1994.

"Hey! Look it here Whitey!" Joe exclaimed as he observed the medieval armor on the walls. " They even have one to put on the horse!"

"Yeah. That they did," Whitey replied. "They had them for horses too."

"Hey Whitey," Joe said as they examined medieval weaponry more closely. "They wore spikes too."

"Hey Yogi. What was the name of that clothing store we worked at?" Whitey asked.

"The American Shop," Yogi replied.

"American Shop," Whitey repeated.

"We'll set them up in there," Yogi joked. "We worked out of there." Yogi pointed at the suits of armor, remembering their work environment in the off-season was like working in a dungeon. Two of the greatest MLB players in history joked about having a second job in the winter to pay the bills. At the same time MLB players in 1994 were complaining about the millions they were already making, while they let down the fans.

"Yeah... I worked," Whitey said. "I used to work there on my day off."

"Ha, ha... did you here what Whitey said?" Mrs. Berra asked. "This shoe store. This place looks like the American Shop." Mrs. Berra laughed.

"The American Shop Joe," Whitey recalled.

Yogi Berra's Last Game

"Oh! Yeah, yeah!" Joe exclaimed. "I remember that."

"We used to work it. I was in the army. I'd go from Fort Monmouth to Newark and they'd pay me fifty bucks for two hours or three hours in the store," Whitey said shaking his head. "That was a lot of money back then."

"Damn right it was a lot of money!" Joe remarked.

"I worked with Phil in the winter time there one year," Yogi recalled.

"American Shop?" Whitey asked.

"American Shop," Yogi replied.

"I use to get ninety-four salary and I'd get two hundred a month working the American Shop," Whitey reflected. They all laughed. Yogi and Whitey, with their playing abilities and stats, would have been two of the highest paid MLB players in 1994, if that had been the era they played in.

158   Yogi Berra's Last Game

It's ironic that two Yankees Hall of Fame icons, with sixteen World Series rings between them, talked about how much or actually how little they earned in the prime of their Major League Baseball careers, while at the very moment of this conversation MLB owners and players were striking over the millions they were making.

"There's an arrow up there!" Yogi enthusiastically observed, as his attention was directed back to the medieval weaponry.

"Where's the ammunition?" a lady in the group asked.

"There's a cannon over there," Yogi remarked. "There's a little cannon over there." He walked towards it to get a better look.

"There's guns on the other side," Whitey remarked.

"They have cannons?" a guy in the group asked.

"Over there... yeah." Whitey said laughing. "It looks like the Hessian army."

"You mean miniatures," the guy said.

"Yeah, they got little cannons," Whitey replied. Whitey examined the medieval weapons hung from the walls and ceiling.

Yogi Berra's Last Game

A short time later Phil finally arrived and Whitey escorted him to see the suits of armor and medieval weapons.

"Phil… look at the American Shop," Whitey joked. He armed Phil with a spear and pointed him towards the suits of armor.

"Hey... we gonna go in there?" Phil asked, who was unaware of what Whitey had planned for him, since he missed the conversations and jokes during his absence. "Yeah! I wanta go back by the armor."

"Here we go!" Phil exclaimed. He charged with the spear toward the suits of armor.

He changed the spear from his right to left hand as he got closer to the armor. "How bout this one?" Phil bragged jokingly. "Left-handed!"

Phil examined the spikes on the end of spear he held. "Oh man!" Phil exclaimed. "This is… you could hit them anyplace with this and you got em!"

Yogi Berra's Last Game

Phil laughed along with his Yankees teammates as they left behind the spears and armor of Castle Kreuzenstein.

They walked through castles that day where armored knights had wielded swords, shields and spears defending their castle and kingdom. Yogi, Whitey, and Phil were knights in their day and risked their lives to defeat Germany, Japan and North Korea in wars.

When those wars were over they wielded wooden baseball bats like steel swords and leather gloves like shields to defeat their baseball rivals. They defended a castle called Yankees Stadium in the Kingdom of MLB, for a city called New York. They were gladiators of their day to millions.

Chapter 6

The Last Game

"I'm Yogi Berra. I'm sixty-nine years old. I played with the NY Yankees for seventeen years. I was in fourteen World Series as a player and we won ten world championships," Yogi stated.

"Hello everyone. I am Whitey Ford. I pitched for the NY Yankees for eighteen years. I won two hundred and thirty six games and lost a hundred and six. I won ten games in the World Series, which I was lucky enough to play in. I had a wonderful career with the NY Yankees," Whitey stated.

"Hi everyone in Austria. My name is Phil Rizzuto. I'm seventy-seven years old, believe it or not. Born in Brooklyn but played with the NY Yankees for sixteen years, ten World Series and I was just the most valuable player this year in nineteen ninety-four. Thank you very much!" Phil remarked.

The work of NY Yankees Hall of Fame Major League Baseball legends never ends when it comes to autographs. A carnival-like atmosphere permeated the field before the game. Fans were everywhere seeking an autograph and a handshake of a lifetime.

"The big pen. That's what we need for the hat," Phil said as he

"I'm Yogi Berra. I'm sixty-nine years old. I played with the NY Yankees for seventeen years. I was in fourteen World Series as a player and we won ten world championships," Yogi stated.

autographed baseballs for the Austrian kids. "I tell yah. I'm nice and warm this way." Austrian kids surrounded him and inadvertently blocked the chilly September wind. "If yah get that pen I'll sign your hat," Phil said.

"Thank you," the Austrian boy said politely.

"You're welcome," Phil replied.

"How are you?" asked the Austrian player.

"Alright," Yogi replied as he stood near home plate. "How you doing?"

An Austrian player walked over with a floppy poster for Yogi to sign. "Oh boy! Look at this... A big one!" Yogi exclaimed as he fumbled with the poster in the wind.

"Hey! How yah doing tiger? Do you get the ballgames over here?" Phil asked as he stood near the dugout.

"Do you watch the ballgame on TV?"

"No," said the Austrian boy.

A fan walked up to Yogi and handed him their ball glove to autograph. He also cradled several baseballs in the other hand. "Look at all the balls this guy got!" Yogi exclaimed as he autographed the glove.

"Hi! How yah doing?" Phil asked as he signed an autograph for an Austrian guy.

"Fine," the Austrian replied. "And you?"

"Good," Phil replied. "Do you play ball?"

"Yes. I'm playing," the Austrian replied.

"Listen. We're gonna need…" Phil began to say.

"I can help you do the homerun, so I can catch it," the Austrian said as he laughed.

"No… Ha, ha. But we need some players, so you kids stick around," Phil said bemused by the language barrier. "Alright?"

"Yes," the Austrian replied.

"Good!" Phil exclaimed.

"No problem," the Austrian replied.

"What happened to the line here?" Phil asked, as the line to get his autograph became a crowd.

"Yeah. Come on guys. Why don't we form a line?" a guy next to Phil asked. "This way you can go one after the other. It'll be a lot easier."

Bill White and the other Yankees players were loosening their throwing arms for the game. Bill tossed a ball to Yogi. He snagged the ball from the air and threw it in one motion. Yogi was a masterful catcher and snagged a lot of balls to win 1951, 1954 and 1955 American League MVP Awards. He was elected to the Hall of Fame in 1972 claiming 339 out of 396 ballots. Yogi Berra struck out just 414 times in more than 8,300 plate appearances over 19 seasons, which is an astonishingly small ratio for a power hitter.

Yogi Berra's Last Game

167

Yogi tentatively stretched his right arm above his head diagnosing it. "I haven't been able to do that for two years," Yogi told Bill.

Yogi continued to nurse his arm when a young boy approached him with a ball to autograph. He immediately reached for the ball and autographed it for the boy.

"Will you bunt in the game Mr. Rizzuto?" an Austrian boy asked.

"I certainly will. I can't hit anymore," Phil joked. "Where'd you read about that bunting?"

"It will be a great day!" the Austrian boy exclaimed.

"It's gonna be an excellent day!" a guy near Phil exclaimed. "The sun's coming out. It's getting warmer."

"How did you know I was a bunter?" Phil asked.

"Huh?" the Austrian boy asked.

"How did you know that I was a bunter?" Phil asked again slowly.

"That's obvious… Ha, ha," the Austrian boy replied.

"Okay," Phil replied bemused as he laughed. "Here… I'll sign the hat with this," Phil said. "Can I borrow your pen one second?"

"Thank you," another Austrian boy said as Phil autographed his hat.

"You're welcome," Phil replied as he gave the pen back. "Thank you very much."

A girl approached Phil for an autograph.

"And how are you today?" Phil asked the girl. "Softball?"

"No… Baseball," the girl stated.

"Baseball!" Phil exclaimed. "No kidding!"

"Ha, ha, ha," the girl giggled.

"I heard Scooter," Phil said.

"Yeah," a boy replied.

"Ha, ha, ha. How yah doing?" Phil asked.

"Good," the boy said.

"Look at the size of this guy!" Phil exclaimed as a tall Austrian player walked up to him for an autograph. "Holy cow! You're not pitching today?"

"No. I'm playing first base," the Austrian player replied.

"Okay… Good," Phil said relieved. "Boy o' boy."

"He is huge," a man commented to Phil after the big guy left.

"He is a big…" Phil said as he autographed a ball. Another Austrian player walked up for an autograph. "Here's a normal guy right here," Phil commented.

"Ballpark News. What is that?" a man asked the Austrian player as he handed Phil the magazine to autograph.

"Yeah… that's ah… Austrian baseball magazine," he replied.

"Oh yeah," Phil replied.

"I'm the chief," he said.

"Yeah… oh geez," Phil replied.

"Okay… I got a pen here," Yogi said as a boy handed him a ball to autograph. Yogi signed the ball and handed it back to the boy. "There you go," Yogi said. Another boy handed him a cap to sign. "Geez… I wish I had the other…" Yogi said as he signed the cap. "It don't write too good on there." A little boy dressed in a baseball jersey and cap brought him an autograph book to sign. Yogi took the book and signed his name.

"Thanks," the boy said.

"What do you think?" I asked.

"Think of what?" Yogi replied as he handed an autographed ball back to a fan. He was quite the character behind home plate. Yogi had a reputation as a talker who attempted to take opposing batters off their game. During the 1958 World Series, Yogi kept telling Hank Aaron to "hit with the label up on the bat". Aaron finally turned and said "Yogi, I came up here to hit, not to read".

Yogi Berra's Last Game

"Are you having fun," I asked?

"Yeah... it's alright," Yogi replied with a smile. "The suns out. It's warmer anyhow." Yogi once said, "It ain't the heat it's the humility."

He looked at his watch. "We still got three and a half hours yet before the game," he remarked. "Two o'clock... two o'clock."

"Lot's of time to figure out what we're doing," I said.

"I don't know," Yogi replied. He once said, "It gets late early out here."

Meanwhile, a crowd of fans stood around Phil waiting for him to autograph the piece of memorabilia they had chose.

"You know what you do... you sign it right on the picture," Phil instructed an Austrian guy holding the Austrian Cup game program opened to Phil's picture. "And that way you know... see."

"I know," the Austrian guy replied. "Only Whitey Ford I missed."

"He's here," Phil commented.

"Yeah... I know... that's him I think," the Austrian guy said, as he pointed at a picture of Whitey in the game program Phil was signing.

"That's Whitey," Phil interrupted pointing at his picture. "Yeah?"

"I thought this was him," the Austrian guy replied.

"Oh no... that's Jackie Jensen," Phil said as he noticed his own picture in the magazine. "Oh... look at me... the Scooter! Alright!"

"Baseball at it's best!" the guy exclaimed.

"Yeah," Phil replied. "Actually… that's a real dumb picture you know… jumping up in the air and catching it down there. But that's the one they use as my rookie card."

A short time later Phil walked out to the field to warm up. He posed for a picture with some kids and noticed the smallest boy was standing out of the picture frame. "Get right here in front of me," Phil told him. "That a boy!"

"Alright!" the boys exclaimed as the camera went off. "Thank you!"

"Okay," Phil replied.

I was about to interview Bill White when Karl Hofer, the Austrian game promoter, handed Bill a Chemical Bank cap to wear.

"I own Chemical Bank stocks and that's alright," Bill said with a grin. "He won't mind that, will he?"

"Who do you think is going to win today?" I asked.

"I think the Chemical Bank guys are gonna win today! Charlie

McCabe will like that!" Bill exclaimed laughing. "No, these kids look like they can play a little bit. We ah... obviously haven't been uh, playing. First time I picked up a bat and glove in about twenty years so ah... it'll be interesting ah... But we'll be fortified by a couple of young kids so we'll be presentable. Yogi's gonna manage us. He's gonna DH for us and every time we get somebody on base we're gonna send our DH up. Ha, ha, ha."

"Hey what are you going to do right after the game?" I asked.

"I am going to Wyer and we're gonna catch a lot of trout. I understand it's one of the nicest spots in upper Austria. It's about two miles from here up in the mountains and we're gonna catch some trout on some flies. I hope they got the right flies up there for me because mine are all ah... They only catch American fish," Bill said as he laughed and took off the Chemical Bank cap. "Okay." Bill White came into baseball as a player in the early days of the game's integration. He was a five-time All-Star first baseman and won seven straight Gold Gloves from 1960-1966 during a 13-year career in which he played for the Cardinals, Giants and Phillies. He is one of the few MLB players who hit at least .300 and drove in at least 100 runs in three consecutive seasons. In 1971 Bill joined the New York Yankees' broadcast team and called Yankee games from 1971 to 1988, most often teamed with Phil Rizzuto and Frank Messer. He did the team's broadcasts on both radio and television during most of that stretch. Bill was the first African-American to do play-by-play regularly for a major-league sports team. He became the National League President in 1989 in a unanimous vote, becoming the first African-American to hold such a high executive position in sports. He was NL president through 1994 during this game, while the MLB Strike was ongoing and cancellation of the World Series had been decided.

Meanwhile Phil and John Moore warmed up and played catch before the game.

"How do you like that glove?" John asked.

"Too big!" Phil shouted. "I got no feel… I'll use it anyway." He threw the ball back to Moore.

"This is about my distance right here… just about here," Phil said as he observed John. "Don't get your arm tired now Moore!"

"My arm will be tired after four pitches anyway," Moore replied.

"Well don't throw too hard… you know… unless you have to," Phil instructed. "You get any men on base… then you throw hard." Phil caught the ball John threw to him. "That's no good if I can't catch em like that! Look there's no feeling in it!" Phil shouted. "Too big!" Phil threw the ball back to John. "Ha, ha, ha…I could never use a glove like this in my life! The pocket goes this way," he explained as he demonstrated with his hand. Phil looked inside the pocket of the glove to see whose model he wanted to get rid of. "Jose Canseco!" Phil shouted with a jokingly.

"Let me take that glove for yah and I'll see if I can get yah a smaller one," a guy said. He walked over to take the glove from Phil.

"Let me hold it till you get another one," Phil said. "Cause I wanta warm up a little." John threw the ball to Phil. "Hey that's one of our players!" Phil exclaimed as he caught the ball and watched the player run by. "It said New York on it." The player was one of the Austrians who were there to help the team Phil was told about when he and the other Yankees met the Mayor. He was wearing a Yankees road gray jersey. Phil threw a few more times to loosen up his arm. "Damn! The arm won't do what I want it to!" He threw the ball back to John with a grimace and walked towards shortstop to test what his throwing distance would be.

Yogi Berra's Last Game

"Now listen Moore... there's gonna be some plays!" Phil shouted.

"I'm ready!" Moore shouted.

"You gotta be ready. Now you make believe... you get on the... near the pitchers mound there!" Phil shouted while he walked to shortstop. "If I get a ground ball sometimes... because I can't reach first base and I... that's it... be ready to throw to first... yes... okay!" Phil shouted as he caught Moore's throw.

"Try it again! Try it again!" Phil shouted. "I'm gonna get the ground ball here." He simulated catching a grounder and threw the ball to Moore. "Oh perfect... perfect!" Phil exclaimed. "Now don't forget, I'm serious."

"That's great for my arm!" Moore shouted back.

"Well let's just see how far I can throw. Don't go too far first... back up after each throw!" Phil shouted as he threw the ball to Moore. "Nope! I know it!" Phil exclaimed as he gingerly stretched his arm and shoulder. "The old arm muscles won't stretch."

Phil created a minor controversy in 1995, scolding Yankees' manager Buck Showalter for not giving rookie shortstop Derek Jeter more playing time. When the New York Daily News named Phil the Yankees' all-time best shortstop in 2003, "The Scooter" complained that Jeter was better, or at least deserved a tie.

Yogi Berra's Last Game

While Phil and John played catch I noticed Joe Pignatano warming up for the game and walked over to interview him.

"How's the other team look?" I asked.

"How does the other team look?" Joe answered, repeating my question. "I don't know… haven't seen em play yet! They don't throw the ball too badly. I mean some of them still need a little work. They need a lot of work. See some of them don't throw the ball too well but some of them throw the ball well. I haven't seen em swing a bat. Some of then handle a glove good… some don't. But like anything else… ah... somebody that's just starting they're gonna have to work at it… and I'm sure we can help em," Joe commented.

"Do you want to win the cup?" I asked.

"I could care less! I don't want to carry that cup home! It's to heavy... that's number one. In fact it's here... let it stay here! It's all right with me. It's not whether we win or lose. It's not whether we win here. If we lose... I think it's great! I think it'd be great for these people right here... but I don't know how the rest of them feel about it. Doesn't bother me one bit. We can leave that cup right here!" Joe exclaimed.

"I hate to get chapped lips... you know." Phil commented as someone helped get Chap Stick from his jacket. "I got my own valet here today." A short time later Phil noticed a very young fan and walked over to meet him. He bent down and gently shook the boys hand.

"Do you want me to sign that ball? Scooter," Phil said to teach the boy his nickname.

Yogi Berra's Last Game

Phil signed the ball and handed it back to the tiny hands.

"Danke," the boy replied. Phil patted the boy's head and reached down to him with his hand.

"Give me five," Phil said.

The boy's tiny hand gently slapped Phil's.

"That a boy... you see that!" Phil exclaimed. "The kid knows what he's doing!"

Phil helped children at St. Joseph's School for the Blind by raising and donating millions until his death.

John and I walked over to the dugout where Yogi stood talking and waited to interview him.

"How was your trip to Vienna?" John asked.

"Oh great!" Yogi exclaimed laughing, "I'm freezing my cajones off!"

"What's the game plan?" John asked.

"I don't know yet." Yogi replied. "We gotta see."

Yogi Berra's Last Game

"Where's Phil at?" Yogi asked. "Why don't you get Phil here?"

"He's around the corner," someone in the dugout said.

"Doing what?" Yogi asked skeptically.

"Trying to get warm," John replied.

Yogi started laughing.

"Is Cora out here now? Yogi asked.

"Yeah," John said. "They just got here."

"They just got here," Yogi repeated.

"How did you like the Vienna Boys Choir?" John asked.

"Oh they were great!" Yogi exclaimed. " Boy... I'd love to hear them again. They were real good."

"How was playing ball with them?" John asked.

"Yeah... They came out and played with us out in the yard out there. It was a lot of fun," Yogi replied.

Yogi Berra's Last Game

"It was a very enjoyable day. Real good." Yogi replied sincerely.

"How was the trip overall?" John asked.

"So far it's great," Yogi replied.

"Do you like the city?" John asked.

"Yeah… nothing wrong with it," Yogi replied with a grin.

He pointed at the Austrian team running on to the field. "They're taking infield now," Yogi said. A serious expression appeared on his face as he observed the players from the Austrian team.

"Did they take infield before?" I asked.

Yogi Berra's Last Game

"I don't know... is that the team we're playing... or is that an all star team?" Yogi asked as he laughed. The Austrian team looked strong with all their young players.

"This is such a big event here," John remarked.

"They're doing alright... selling a lot of balls. They sold out," Yogi remarked. "They sold out on the balls."

"Everyone wants to go away with a souvenir," John replied.

"I know it. You got a lot of Americans here too," Yogi remarked. "A lot of Americans." He once said, "If the people don't want to come out to the ballpark, nobody's going to stop them." The fans came out for this game.

Yogi managed the Yankees to the 1964 World Series but was fired after losing the seven game series to the Cardinals. He came back to manage the Yankees in 1984, for Steinbrenner, only to be fired again.

187

"What do you think of these guys?" John asked. "Seen anything yet?"

"No… I haven't seen anything yet," Yogi replied with a grin as he looked out onto field. "Our guys are over there hitting."

Yogi Berra's Last Game

"You're signing so many autographs you won't be able to throw a ball later on," I remarked.

"I can't throw anyhow," Yogi replied as he laughed. "I'm too old."

"I really miss your broadcast," a lady said.

"Oh… so do I," Phil replied. "Where are yah from?"

"New York," she replied.

"Where?" Phil asked.

"Ah… Westchester," she replied. "It's kind of embarrassing to start your child on baseball and then baseball folds up."

"Yeah… Isn't that something!" Phil exclaimed.

A short time later Phil was tossing the ball when John and I walked over to interview him.

"How has your Vienna trip been?" John asked.

"I'll tell yah…it's really been an education. It's tough with these language barriers because they told me that most people spoke English here in Austria and Vienna but… ah… it's hard to find English speaking people. We make ourselves known and actually we make ourselves known because we're so loud… but when you talk to them, finally they know what you're trying to say. Every place we've gone the enthusiasm for baseball really seems to have caught on here. These kids that have done such a great job here with this first baseball team and this first baseball field. In Austria this is the first baseball field that they've ever had and these kids built it all themselves. You gotta give them a hand for that. I mean they really did a great job. I've enjoyed it. We've seen some sights, some beautiful castles and monuments. The Vienna Choir Boys were outstanding! But yah know one thing… when we sang "Take Me Out To The Ballgame" to them they weren't to impressed but ah… it was just the idea of singing to them.

> *Every place we've gone the enthusiasm for baseball really seems to have caught on here. These kids that have done such a great job here with this first baseball team and this first baseball field. In Austria this is the first baseball field that they've ever had and these kids built it all themselves. You gotta give them a hand for that.*

I don't think anybody's sung to them unless it was Pavarotti or somebody. I thought we did an excellent job," Phil remarked.

190   Yogi Berra's Last Game

"How was meeting the Mayor of Vienna?" John asked.

"That was very exciting too. It looked like Lindsey Nelson sports jacket that he had on but it was very sharp and he gave me a beautiful little memento of Vienna," Phil replied. Lindsey Nelson was an American sportscaster best known for his broadcasts of New York Mets baseball.

"How did you like the Castle Kreuzenstein?" John asked.

"I tell yah… that was very interesting and the stories they told about that Richard the Lion Hearted. It looked more like Dracula's castle. I figured Igor was coming out any minute," Phil replied.

"Have you been surprised with the enthusiasm for baseball in Austria?" John asked.

"I really have," Phil replied. "I mean… you know over here soccer is their big sport. They call it football but it is soccer. You see the kids here now with the Cubs uniform on, Yankees hats, Atlanta Braves… it's great to see that! Once they get an idea of what all the other sports are all about they'll take to it."

"How long has it been since you played on the field?" John asked.

"Very long time! Very long time!" Phil exclaimed. "It should be very interesting today this game cause nobody's gonna be able to reach first base. Don't know if we'll be able to catch the ball and throw them out but we're gonna give it our best. It's going to be interesting. I have some trepidation in facing these kids. That one kids a pretty fast pitcher I understand… and the old reflexes aren't quite there. But I tell yah… I'm glad I came. I never thought it would be this impressive or pleasant."

"What are your thoughts on the MLB strike?" John asked.

Yogi Berra's Last Game

"Oh... isn't that awful! I mean that strike!" Phil exclaimed. "I'm glad I'm out of the states! I can't stand to read all that stuff! Both these sides... the owners and the players are really dumb! I gotta say that real loud so they hear it!"

The 1994 baseball strike was the biggest ever in professional sports history. The strike resulted in a loss of money for the owners and players and created disillusionment for fans. The number of participants were about 750 players and 28 owners which is not large, so each had a lot at stake. The strike brought baseball to a halt and America's pastime didn't return until 1995. It ended Tony Gwynn's potential .400 season and Michael Jordan's baseball career. Bo Jackson and Goose Gossage never played another major league game again.

"They have ruined what could have been the greatest year in baseball... and it's gonna be tough to duplicate it and it's gonna hurt baseball too. Right now nobody's interested whether they play the World Series or not... and right now they've had to cancel the World Series, so there'll be no World Series, first one since 1904," Phil replied as he pondered for a moment. "The old timers really feel bad about it. The young kids... ah... I mean they're making a lot of money and I imagine they're gonna hold out a long, long time... But the time is gonna come when they'll really want to play ball and get back in the swing of things. Baseball is in a very precarious spot right now. I'm anxious to see what's gonna happen next year."

> *...and right now they've had to cancel the World Series, so there'll be no World Series, first one since 1904," Phil replied as he pondered for a moment.*

"Have you been out to Monument Park?" John asked jokingly comparing the Yankees stadium memorial park for Babe Ruth and other Yankees legends to the Austrian ballpark with the sponsor signage.

"I'll tell yah, they did such a great job the kids. They must a worked all day and all night to get up the balloons and the big cans and the temporary seats they got there and the concession stands. I tell yah... I think it's wonderful!" Phil exclaimed. He quickly gazed around the field. "I always said that through sports you can cement relationships with different countries better than any other thing. Politics never seem to work. Just get the athletes over there and they can break through anything." "You'd be surprised how much sports can do to help the men who have just returned from battle," Phil told The Sporting News in November 1944.

Whitey Ford was on the field warming up before the game.

"What do you think of the strike?" I asked.

"That is the saddest thing I've ever had in my life as far as baseball. First of all... I still work for the NY Yankees and I thought we were gonna be in a World Series finally after many years and players like Don Mattingly and ah... fella's like that finally had a chance to play in the World Series and it's not gonna happen and I feel really bad about that," Whitey stated. "I'm mad at both of them. I wish they would each give... you know? The owners give a little, the players give a little and get back to playing baseball. But I'm afraid there's not gonna be any baseball till maybe next April or May."

Former Cardinal first baseman and current NL president Bill White sat in the dugout when I walked over to him.

"What are your thoughts on the game?" I asked.

"We're gonna get killed!" Bill exclaimed as he laughed. "Forty years ago we could do it… but now I'm sixty, Phil's in his seventies, Yogi's in his late sixties, Whitey's in his late sixties and it's gonna be tough. But I think when you make a trip like this… This obviously breaks the ice. Everybody wants to see Rizzuto, they want to see Berra, they want to see Ford and they want to see Slaughter. I think the next time, when we do come over, we'll have some kids that can make the double plays... who can do the things that these kids need to see in order for them to become better."

Phil was sitting in the dugout signing autographs when a guy handed him a book to autograph.

Yogi Berra's Last Game

"Oh, you know... This is a good book. Is that the Yankee one?" Phil asked as he autographed the guy's book. "The Bronx Zoo?"

"Yeah," the guy replied.

"Yeah... that's really a good book!" Phil exclaimed. "Good pictures in there... right?"

"Yeah," the guy replied as Phil signed the book.

"But look at this... what you got on?" Phil asked as he noticed the guy's cap. "You huckleberries! You got the Mets there!" The guy laughed at Phil's comment as Phil handed him back the book.

"Thanks," the guy said.

"You're welcome," Phil replied. Phil dropped his pen and a boy picked it up from the dugout floor and handed it to him.

"Thank you very much young man!" Phil exclaimed. "You go to school over here?"

"Yeah," the boy said.

"Are yah from the states?' Phil asked.

"Yeah," the boy replied.

"Where?" Phil asked.

"Ah... Seattle," the boy replied.

"Oh... I love that city!" Phil exclaimed. "Yah see where they're not gonna be able to play? They wouldn't been able to play any more games the rest of the year."

"Yeah," the boy said.

"It's a shame too," Phil said. "Griffey was having some year."

"Everyone was," the boy said.

"I love Seattle. I mean the... the ah... scenery and the ah..." Phil said..

"So what do yah think of the strike?" the boy asked.

"Oh... terrible! Absolutely terrible!" Phil exclaimed. "Worst thing that could've happened! I never thought it would... I thought maybe at the

197

most it might last four or five days but…"

"You still doing broadcast?" a lady listening nearby asked.

"Yes," Phil replied.

"Still working?" the lady inquired.

"Yup," Phil replied. "Well right now I'm not working."

"This is pleasure," the lady commented referring to the ball game.

"What's today's date?" Phil asked.

"Today's the eighteenth," the lady replied.

"The eighteenth," Phil repeated. "That's right… the season still has time to go."

"Do you think that strike will be settled before spring training?" a man nearby asked.

"No… I don't think so," Phil replied. "I really don't. I think that ah… I hope it's settled. I mean… it's ridiculous if it's not though."

"Yeah," the lady commented. "That's the first time since 1904."

"Yup," Phil replied.

"How do you like Vienna?" the lady asked.

"I love it… I love it!" Phil exclaimed. "I wish it was a little warmer cause walking around there's so many nice things… But it got a little chilly there in the last couples of days."

"You had a worse winter than they we had here last winter," the lady remarked.

"Oh yeah!" Phil exclaimed. "Every three days… every three days… it would be first sleet and ice and snow… and it would be covered up… and you could never get rid of the ice."

"Excuse me Mr. Rizzuto," a young woman interrupted. "Would you please sign my ball?"

"Sure," Phil replied.

"Thank you very much," she said.

"Do you play the softball game?" Phil asked as he autographed her ball. "They have some girl's softball teams I understand."

"Yeah... I am on the softball team," she said.

"Oh... are yah," Phil replied. "Oh."

"I'm the centerfielder," she said.

"Oh, no kidding!" Phil exclaimed. "Who's the one that pitches real fast?"

"Kristina... where are they," she asked herself as she looked around.

"Are they here?" Phil asked. "I heard she could really pitch."

"Yeah... she's a good one!" she remarked.

"How do you do with the hitting?" Phil asked.

"I'm okay," she said. "I'm okay."

"Yeah..." Phil replied.

A guy in line for an autograph walked up to Phil with a book to sign. Phil opened the book and noticed a picture.

"I remember this base hit right over Newcomb's head," Phil said. "Yeah... I never saw this one before. The head I mean. I remember as soon as I saw Newcomb duck in there it went right through the middle." Phil turned the pages of the book and came across one that made him stop. "What is this one up here?" Phil asked pointing at a picture.

"Forty-nine," the guy replied.

"Oh yeah... that was a great year! I had a good year that year. Holy cow!" Phil exclaimed. "That brings back memories... brings back memories.

"You had a lineup today boy... lot of kids," a guy said referring to the number of autographs Phil signed. "That little boy was so cute.

"Here he is," Phil said as he noticed the boy. "Is that yours?"

"Yes," the woman replied.

"Oh, he is so cute!" Phil exclaimed. "He gave me five!"

She brought the boy closer to Phil.

"Hi, I met you Stephan before. Remember you gave me... give me five." Phil coaxed the tired toddler as he extended his hand to him. "Boy it's getting a little chilly."

"Yup," the woman replied.

"All of a sudden," Phil said. "It was so nice and warm." He looked up at the sky. "Oh, look at that cloud that's up there! I think I'm gonna stay in the dugout. Gonna try and stay warm. Man it's cold!"

"We're gonna take a little infield in awhile," a guy told Phil. "Okay?"

"I can't reach first base," Phil stated. "I've been trying to reach first base."

"Throw it to second," the guy said.

"I got to get a smaller glove," Phil said. "This is so big. I can't... no feel."

"I couldn't play with them," Enos said nearby on the dugout bench.

"I can't," Phil said. "This is to big."

"I'll find yah a smaller glove," the guy said.

"Hey Phil!" another guy shouted out. "Scooter!"

"What?" Phil answered.

"We got a glove for yah," the guy said.

"Where?" Phil asked.

"Right here," the guy replied.

Ralph Branca looked at the glove Phil was offered.

"I don't know if this is much smaller," Ralph said as he examined the glove.

"It is smaller," Phil said. "We got to find out whose that is."

"He's gonna see you after, when you come off the field," Larry replied. "You give it to him."

"Yeah... But that one I was supposed to autograph," Phil replied. "You know who it is?"

"I'll find out," Larry replied. "I'll get it to the coach and he'll give it to him."

Yogi Berra's Last Game

"Oh look… they're taking infield!" Phil exclaimed. "Is that our team? I'm supposed to be taking infield practice. They're taking infield practice without us Moore. I can't believe it!"

"I'm a pitcher," Moore said.

"Oh… that's right," Phil said.

A short time later Phil and John took a walk to the restroom.

"My mich's on. They're hearing all this," Phil said as he tried to relieve himself.

"Live too," John joked.

"Live from Vienna!" Phil announced as he laughed.

Meanwhile, Enos Slaughter sat on the dugout bench signing autographs when he noticed me filming him.

"Surprised to see all the people. I'm glad to see them come out cause I think that it'll help baseball, you know… over here in Austria," Enos commented. "It seems like they got a lot of enthusiasm and I think everything's gonna work out great! I'm real happy to be here to contribute whatever I may… to this baseball here in Austria."

"Did you enjoy the Vienna Boys Choir," I asked?

"Oh… The Vienna Choirboys… yeah! We had quite a time the other night!" Enos exclaimed. "If the sun would come out it'd be a little better. This cold weather… I don't like to play this game in cold weather cause my blood has done gotten a little thin now."

Most great players have something similar during their careers, a dominant year, a key series in which they made their name, or a signature play. Enos Slaughter's even had a nickname. His "Mad Dash" in Game Seven of the 1946 World Series took place on the brightest of stages. In the bottom of the eighth Enos took off from first with the pitch. He recklessly ran through a stop sign at third and charged home. Enos scored the game winning run from first on a single. The tough old Hall of Fame legend sat in the dugout of this game in Austria trying to stay warm.

Phil sat down next to Bill White when he came back to the dugout.

"They have to clear the field. They said," Phil commented. "I think the show is gonna start pretty soon."

"Cora told me to deliver a message," a lady said to Phil as she approached him in the dugout.

"What?" Phil asked.

"They don't have anything hot to drink but, they have wine and it's not that strong," the lady replied.

"Forget it!" Phil exclaimed.

"She wants to know if you want to..." the lady began to say.

"No thank you," Scooter replied. "Tell my bride that I'm an athlete and I don't drink alcohol on the day of the game!"

A short time later Phil reminisced with Bill.

"My home town," Phil said.

"I thought you said you were from Hillside," Bill said.

Yogi Berra's Last Game

"Well, I mean now that's my adopted town but, where I was born is not far from Ebbets Field," Phil replied.

"Where?" Bill asked.

"In Ridgewood, New York," Phil replied.

"What?" Bill asked.

"Ridgewood, it's right near Ebbets Field," Phil replied. "We used to go over there. We went to Ebbets Field more than we went to Yankees stadium."

"I thought you said Richman Hill," Bill commented.

"I went to Richman Hill High School," Phil replied.

"This is the first time I've heard about Ridgewood," Bill replied.

"That's where I was born. Ridgewood. Beautiful little town." He pondered for a moment and sighed, "Oh White. The good old days..." Phil reminisced. Bill began to laugh.

Phil "Scooter" Rizzuto and Bill White formed a famous bond during their magical eighteen year association as broadcasters with the New York Yankees. "None of it was planned," Bill said in his autobiography "Uppity", which is serious except when it recounts the 18 years he worked with Phil. His book should be required reading for an MLB player. "My voice teacher didn't want me to have anything to do with him on the air," said White, who added, "Obviously, I didn't listen." He played off Rizzuto, cementing their partnership. Their magic hadn't been lost as they sat in the dugout before this historical game in Austria. It was quite a day surrounded by men who changed society and created history.

"You gonna play shortstop?" Bill asked.

"No, no... I went from shortstop, tried to throw to first base," Phil replied. "I couldn't reach. I'm switching to second base. Second I think I can reach."

A short time later as Yogi and the guys hung out in the dugout they discussed the Redskins and Giants game playing that evening.

"I'll take the skins," Bill said as he overheard them.

"They got TV?" Yogi asked.

"We got it live," someone said.

"Let's go and watch TV," Yogi said.

"We got it figured out Yog," Phil said.

Joe noticed the graffiti on the wall of the dugout behind Yogi.

"Did you see what he put up there?" Joe asked Yogi.

Yogi Berra's Last Game

"Who… Whitey and I," Yogi replied.

Joe read the freshly written graffiti on the wall of the new dugout.

"Whitey Ford was here nine, eighteen, ninety-four cold sober!" Joe exclaimed. "Yogi Berra was drunk!" Yogi stood in the dugout with his arms folded and laughed at Joe's response. This comical and historical writing of Whitey Ford, Yogi's batterymate, is hopefully saved and framed.

Joe "Piggy" Pignatano appeared in 307 major league games during all or part of six seasons. He was a catcher for the Brooklyn Dodgers, Los Angeles Dodgers, Kansas City Athletics and New York Mets from 1957-62. Joe coached with the Washington Senators, NY Mets and Atlanta Braves. He earned two World Series rings, one with the "69" Miracle Mets.

"That damn Whitey, he's to much," Joe said shaking his head.

Yogi looked for a response from Phil and Bill who were talking and just smiled. Someone mentioned Joe Dimaggio and Marilyn Monroe in the dugout.

"Yeah!" Phil exclaimed. "He was talking about DiMaggio and Marilyn Monroe!"

"You don't want to talk about that," Bill commented.

"I didn't want any part of that," Phil replied, who had been Dimaggio's roommate on Yankees road trip games.

"I don't know if it's good for baseball, but it sure beats the hell out of rooming with Phil Rizzuto," said Yogi Berra about the marriage of Joe Dimaggio and Marilyn Monroe.

A short time later Yogi and Phil examined the length of the aluminum

Yogi Berra's Last Game

bats with Bill.

"Think you can lay one down with that one?" someone asked.

"That's little league," Bill observed as Phil held the bat.

"Yeah, that is little league," Phil agreed. "I've never hit with one. You?"

"Me either," Yogi said.

"You White?" Phil asked.

"I don't think so," Bill replied. "I can't remember."

"We'll use this one," Yogi decided. "You think we can hit it." Yogi began to survey the field of Austrian players warming up.

Yogi coached for the Houston Astros starting in 1985 and retired in 1992 which ended his 46 years in Major League Baseball. This was his first participation in a ballgame in two years and his last.

A short time later, I handed my Austrian Cup game program to Phil for an autograph.

"Phil maybe knows who they are," Yogi replied as Phil handed him my game program to autograph.

"What? Who's that?" Phil asked.

"Who are the guys that wanta play with us?" Bill asked.

"Our players," Phil replied.

"Yeah," Bill answered.

"On our trip," Phil replied. "Oh, I don't know. I don't know who they are. Karl... see Karl... I think Karl... ah... made money like a..."

"They got some money..." Yogi began to say.

"Ah... tourist thing... you know." Phil finished saying.

"Oh... did he?" Bill asked.

"Yeah. I think," Phil said, regarding the game promoter Karl Hofer.

"And... and... he invited some people?" Bill asked.

"Huh?" Phil replied as he stood and signed his name on the dugout wall.

"He invited some people?" Bill repeated.

"He must have," Phil replied.

"Huh..." Bill replied without missing a beat. "He ought to tell us about it!" Yogi finished autographing my game program and handed it to me.

"Thank you," I said. Bill's concern about Karl was troubling to them. Why didn't Karl tell Yogi, Phil, Bill, Whitey, Enos, Ralph and the other players about tourists paying to play in the game? What was he hiding?

> *"Huh..." Bill replied.*
> *"He ought to tell us about it!"*

Yogi's autograph stands alone in the upper right hand corner just like his baseball career and life. The game program reads Vienna on the cover but the game was played on a Sunday in the village of Stockerau.

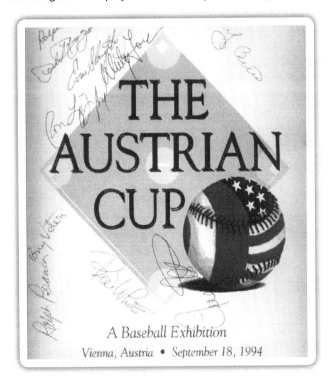

Pre-game entertainment included a military helicopter and martial arts exhibition.

Whitey is now known as "The Greatest Living Yankees" since Yogi passed away. Whitey demonstrated his new karate moves to me.

Yogi Berra's Last Game

Phil was concerned over a choirboy from the Vienna Boys Choir that came to watch the game. Phil promised the choirboy, when he played ball with him earlier in the week, he could sit in the dugout during the game.

"I promised the one kid from the Vienna Boys Choir that he could sit here a little bit... alright," Phil told Karl. "I found him... he came down."

"Yeah," Karl replied. "Cause I kicked everyone out."

"Where is he? Oh here he is... here he is Karl!" Phil exclaimed. "So let him. Let him just sit here... alright... because I promised him." The choirboy sat down and watched the game with Phil and the guys.

A short time later Yogi noticed the red cap Karl persuaded Phil to wear for the game sponsor. Although Yogi hadn't worn a Yankees cap since George Steinbrenner replaced him as Yankees manager in1985, he was getting used to wearing it again in 1994.

"Put on you're right hat and take that hat off!" Yogi told Phil.

"I'm just gonna keep this on. Karl wants me to say something about this Casinos Royale," Phil said. "They're the ones that paid all the money to get us over here… so I just have to put this on in the beginning. Where's the guy with my hat?" Phil meant to say Casinos Austria were the sponsor.

A short time later Yogi, Phil and the others were standing on the field before the game debating who would manage the team.

"Hey White, who's the manager on our club? Phil asked. "You?"

"You," Yogi replied swiftly to Phil attempting to avoid a managing job.

"Yogi," Ralph Branca intervened as swiftly as Yogi's escape attempt.

"Yogi," Bill agreed since Yogi was the only one who'd ever managed.

Yogi punched the catcher's mitt with his fist as Phil walked towards him.

"Look at this damn thing," Yogi remarked disapprovingly.

"That looks like one of your old gloves," Phil concluded.

"Not mine... Joe's," Yogi responded. "I couldn't use this stupid thing!"

"Hey we playing or DHing?" Bill asked unaware of their conversation.

"Hey Phil?" Joe asked as he pointed at the glove in Yogi's hand.

"What?" Phil replied.

"You had to be a catcher to use that," Joe teased to provoke Yogi.

"That's right! That's right! Phil exclaimed as they teased Yogi. "These first baseman's gloves they're using now."

"I need a bigger web," Yogi responded as though he was unaware of Joe and Phil's catcher's comment. "I had a bigger web."

Yogi Berra didn't make an error in 88 games as a catcher in 1958. This made him one of four catchers in history to register a 1.000 fielding percentage for a single season.

"He seemed to be doing everything wrong, yet everything came out

213

right. He stopped everything behind the plate and hit everything in front of it," said Mel Ott of Yogi, who was right fielder for the New York Giants, an All-Star eleven consecutive seasons, and Hall of Fame player with 511 home runs; .304 batting average; 1,860 RBI's and 2,876 hits.

Yogi, Whitey, Phil and the other players lined up for the National Anthem.

"Take off your hat Whitey!" Yogi commanded. Whitey took his cap off and held it patriotically over his heart. The National Anthem didn't begin so Yogi and Whitey put their caps back on. "They screwed up again," Yogi joked as they all laughed alluding to Karl Hofer, the Austrian promoter, who couldn't organize the festivities for the game satisfactorily. Karl was the guy that never told the players he'd invited paying tourists. National

Yogi Berra's Last Game

League President Bill White figured this out earlier talking with Yogi and Phil. Karl kept dropping the ball and "screwing up" like Yogi said.

"Hey Yog," Larry said, regarding game promoter Karl Hofer. "When you're around that man you got to be very, very flexible."

"There's nothing written down on paper or anything," a guy added.

"Wait a minute this sounds like it!" Phil exclaimed. Yogi and Whitey laughed with Phil wondering what was happening next.

"Take off your hat Whitey!" Yogi commanded. Whitey took his cap off and held it patriotically over his heart.

"What'd he say?" Yogi asked regarding the announcers comments.

Yogi Berra's Last Game

While Karl attended to the National Anthem, which delayed the game, Phil and Yogi searched for their wives in the bleachers.

"Where the wives?" Yogi asked Phil as they searched through the crowded bleachers. "Where they got their seats... way up there?"

"No, some are right in the first row here in back of the dugout," Phil replied. "The left of the dugout."

"Well there's the left and I don't see em," Yogi retorted.

"Lancelotti was trying to get all the wives to sit in the dugout!" Phil exclaimed referring to a guy who was assisting Karl on the tour. "But Karl wouldn't let em!"

"The dugout," Yogi repeated.

"Karl wouldn't let em... and they're not together," Phil said, concerned. It was ungracious of Karl not letting the wives sit in the dugout with their husbands, considering the effort they made to support him and the game.

Yogi and Phil walked closer to the crowded bleachers searching for their wives.

"They got to be right nearby... I would think," Phil said. "Down here... maybe you can see them." Yogi and Phil walked closer to the bleachers.

"Do you see Cora?" Yogi asked.

"There's Cora," Phil said relieved.

"Having known Yogi and Carmen for so long, it is almost impossible to imagine two people who complemented each other better than they did." said George Steinbrenner.

As the sky became overcast, Phil looked for his Yankees cap.

"You find the guy with my hat?" Phil asked.

"You think there's gonna be lightning?" Bill asked.

"No. Just a little superstitious... that's all, " Phil replied. "Did you find that guy with my hat?" Phil left the dugout with Yogi for the lineup introduction without his Yankees cap.

"Phil Rizzuto!" the announcer exclaimed. The crowd applauded as Phil ran onto the field. "Enos Slaughter!" the announcer exclaimed. The crowd applauded.

"We got to give em... We got to give em the high!" Phil told Enos as he approached him. "We got to give em the five!"

"Yogi Berra!" the announcer exclaimed. Yogi trotted onto the field in his Yankees road grays. He removed his Yankees cap and waved to the cheering crowd. It was the first time in nearly ten years that the NY Yankees Hall of Fame catcher Yogi Berra had worn the Yankees uniform.

"I like your uniform!" Phil shouted to Yogi. Yogi put his Yankees cap

219

back on and jogged over to his Hall of Fame teammates.

"Whitey Ford!" the announcer exclaimed. Whitey tipped his cap to the crowd as he ran onto the field.

Yogi Berra's Last Game

Phil, Enos and Yogi watched as Whitey trotted towards them onto the field.

"Hey!" Phil exclaimed. "We got to give em the high five when he comes!" Yogi pointed at Whitey's shoes as he approached the lineup. Whitey had worn his dress shoes to play in the game. "Come on! Let's go!" Phil shouted to Whitey. "That a boy!"

"If they hit my hand wrong I'll die," Enos said.

"I like your uniform!" Phil shouted to Yogi.

"Bill White!" the announcer exclaimed. Bill ran onto the field towards the legendary lineup and Whitey greeted him with a high five underhand.

"I don't shake hands much with that hand," Enos said.

"Oh... Whack em!" Phil exclaimed exuberantly to Enos. Yogi, Whitey, Phil and Enos, along with the rest of the team, applauded as the young Austrian players, too fortify the team, joined the Yankees lineup.

"What's his name?" Enos asked.

"He's from the other team," Phil replied. "They're gonna play with us. Another kid... ooh... look at em!" Phil's trepidation seemed to be dissipating knowing they actually had some backup players to help them. Maybe they had a chance to win the last game they ever played in for America and the Americans fans, who came to watch them play.

The Hall of Fame teammates watched the Austrians players lineup.

Yogi Berra's Last Game

After the Austrian players lineup was introduced they ran over and greeted the old guys.

"I used to run like that too!" Enos exclaimed.

"Oh, look at this… wait a minute… not so hard!" Phil exclaimed as he shook hands with a player. "They do it to hard!"

Joe Pignatano walked over and stood in front of the Austrian players and umpire.

"Now, you got a bunch of old men over there! You gotta take it easy when you throw the ball!" Joe instructed, as he looked at the umpire. "And you, make sure you call the right strike!" The old guys laughed as they listened to Joe.

"All I'd say… if they're close enough to call… they're close enough to swing at!" Enos exclaimed to the guys as they all laughed.

Yogi Berra's Last Game

"Hey, look at all the men they got!" Phil remarked. "They got about eighteen!" The Austrian team captain walked towards them. "This… This, is the guy that brought… ah… baseball here. That brought em together," Phil said as the captain approached. "Yog, turn around. He wants to give you a high-five." Yogi turned around and shook hands. Yogi hadn't stood in a lineup to shake hands as a Yankees player, for 31 years, since 1963.

"It's like deja vu all over again," Yogi once said.

Whitey, Enos and Phil stood behind Yogi greeting the players. "Alright! Congratulations!" Phil exclaimed. "Hey! All right! Not to hard like you guys do over there. Nice and easy." The players finished greeting each other and stood in their lineups for the National Anthems of each country.

225

The last time Yogi, Whitey or Enos stood together to sing the National Anthem was before game seven of the 1956 World Series. The Hall of Fame legends placed their caps over their hearts and looked out over the rolling hills of the Austrian countryside to sing the National Anthem. The only National Anthem sung by the only MLB players before the only baseball game in September of 1994.

> *"Now… you got a bunch of old men over there! You gotta take it easy when you throw the ball!" Joe instructed.*

"Ah hah!" Phil exclaimed as he heard the music begin. "Oh say can you see by the dawn's early light. What so proudly we hail," Phil sang. "And the home of the brave!" The National Anthem concluded. "All right now. Keep the hats off," Phil reminded the old guys. "They gotta play theirs now."

The Austrian Anthem began to play and finally concluded.

"I guess that's it. Right," Phil commented.

"Wait, wait," Yogi told Phil. "You gotta a speech to do."

"Where do I do it?" Phil asked as the Austrian team captain began to speak.

Yogi rubbed Dell's baldhead as the speaker finished his speech. Maybe Yogi did it for luck or because he liked to joke around to loosen everybody up. Whatever it was, Yogi and the guys laughed liked hell.

Whitey tugged on Dell's mustache causing Yogi to laugh hysterically. Yogi, at age 37, caught 22 innings of a Yankees against the Tigers in Detroit June 24, 1962. The Yanks won 9-7 after seven hours of play.

Yogi Berra's Last Game

The Austrian team captain continued to introduce the dignitaries that were there for the game.

"What did he say?" Phil asked the Austrian umpire.

"It's our president," the umpire replied.

"Oh yeah… that's right," Phil replied.

"The lady in pink," the umpire said.

"Oh yes… yes, yes," Phil replied as he recognized her. "She's been with us the last several days."

"You have a good time?" the umpire asked.

"Oh great!" Phil exclaimed. "Look how nice and warm it got all of a sudden. I was freezing up to just a little while ago."

"Everybody was," the umpire said.

"Yeah," Phil replied. Yogi and the old guys stood and listened to the Austrian captain's speech.

"A very warm welcome and many thanks to the guys standing to my left. These Hall of Fame players, we really, really appreciate what you are doing here for us! This is the biggest honor for us to have you here for the field opening! I think everyone here appreciates it very much! Thank you!" the Austrian captain exclaimed. Everyone applauded as the Austrian team captain walked over and handed a memento of their appreciation to Phil for each of the Yankees. "Thank you very much for coming," the Austrian Captain said. "We don't have much to give."

"Thank you," Phil said as he accepted the gifts and microphone to speak. The crowd cheered and applauded.

"Listen. He said that it was an honor for them to have us here and it's more than an honor for us to be here. This is historic I think!" Phil remarked. "And we'd like to thank Casinos Royale for bringing us here," Phil stopped talking and examined the microphone. "Is the microphone

Yogi Berra's Last Game

on?" The Austrian captain walked over and checked the microphone. "Oh... nice going Jerry!" Phil exclaimed referring to the comedians Jerry Lewis or maybe Jerry Seinfeld. Everyone laughed as the Austrian captain handed the microphone back to Phil. "Hello... hello... testing," Phil said into the microphone. "Okay... now what did I say?" He looked at Yogi and recalled what he was saying. "We want to thank Casinos Royale for bringing us over here, but also we're so proud of these young men for the job they did on this field. When they told us, when they started to build this. Congratulations and let's have a nice game!"

"Yogi had the fastest bat I ever saw. He could hit a ball late, that was already past him, and take it out of the park. The pitchers were afraid of him because he'd hit anything," said teammate Hector Lopez.

"It's Casinos Austria not Casinos Royale," Yogi told Phil.

"What'd I say?" Phil asked. "Casinos Royale did I say?"

"Yeah," Yogi replied.

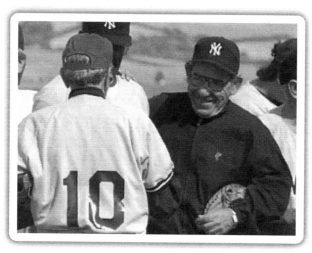

"Well that was the movie," Phil said referring to the 1967 comedy film Casino Royale with David Niven, Ursula Andress and Woody Allen. Yogi laughed as Phil critiqued his own speech. "I know it... I butchered it!" Phil exclaimed. "I was thinking of the movie... Casino Royale!" Yogi grinned.

Yogi Berra's Last Game

"I got to catch the Mayor's first ball," Yogi told Phil as he punched his fist in and out of the glove. He was referring to the ceremonious first pitch.

"Don't miss it," Phil cautioned. "Don't miss it!"

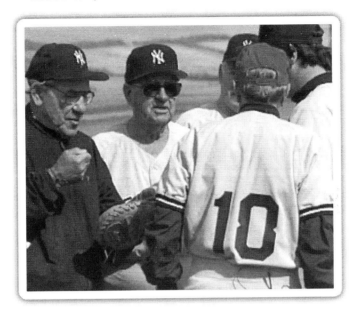

"The Mayor's here," Phil said. Yogi went to home plate where the Mayor of Stockerau waited for him.

"That's not the Mayor. Oh yeah, this mayor. The mayor of this town. Yeah," Phil said as he realized it was not the Mayor of Vienna. "Let's play ball!"

The Mayor threw out the ceremonial first pitch to Yogi at home plate to commemorate the first baseball game played on the field. Yogi leaped off the ground for the poorly thrown ball but couldn't reach it above his head.

"Whoa!" the crowd exclaimed.

Yogi Berra's Last Game

"Oh come on Yog… get off your…" Phil shouted from the dugout!

"Try it again Yog," Whitey yelled. Yogi kicked the air with his foot after he landed and ran to retrieve the ball.

"Go get behind him Phil," someone said to Phil.

"That's what I should have done. That would've been funny," Phil replied. "If he does it again… he's not gonna do it again."

"It went over Yogi's head," Enos said.

Yogi picked up the ball and walked back to the Mayor. They shook hands and posed for a picture with the Austrian team captain.

"Why has our pitching been so great? Our catcher that's why," said Yankees Manager Casey Stengel.

Phil coached his pinch runner from the dugout, as he got ready to hit.

"Now you gonna come and tag me or am I just taking off?" he asked.

"No you can't take off! Let me go a little bit. I'll start out and you just run up to the line and I'll cut this way and you just take off," Phil explained from the dugout. "All right?"

"Whitey's going to first," Ralph said as he sat in the dugout.

"Huh. You want me to go to third?" Enos asked as he sat in the dugout. Meanwhile, Yogi finished with the mayor and trotted back to the

Yogi Berra's Last Game

Yankees dugout.

"Okay Yog!" Enos exclaimed. "Go get em!"

"Who's leading off for us? Where's our lineup?" Phil asked Yogi as he got to the dugout. "Where's the lineup Yog?"

"I don't know," Yogi replied. "I don't have it."

"Well whose got the lineup?" Phil asked.

"You're leading off," Yogi said.

"No... I'm not leading off!" Phil exclaimed.

"Yes you are," Yogi replied. "You're leading off."

"I'm batting second," Phil said. "We only got one bat? How many bats we got? Is this a regular bat... huh?"

"Put a helmet on," Yogi ordered Phil.

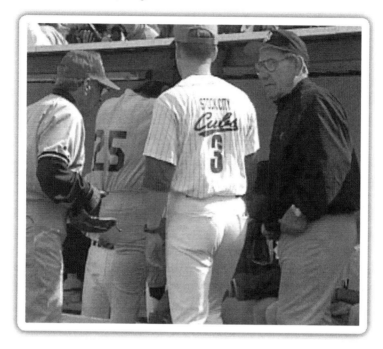

Phil looked through the baseball helmets to find one that would fit.

"I never wore one of these in my life. No, I can't," Phil chuckled.

"Yeah, yeah put it on... leave it on," Joe said as he sat in the dugout.

"Yeah, but I want one a little tighter," Phil said, as he stood just outside the dugout. Phil took that helmet off and looked for another as a bat fell on his foot. "Ow... God damn!" Phil shouted. "It hit me right on my toes!" An Austrian player handed a helmet to Phil. "Is that a small one?" Phil asked.

"What you need is a square one," Ralph Branca teased from the dugout.

"I heard that," Phil said as he struggled to pull the helmet over his head.

"I think this is better... that's good," Phil said as he finally got a helmet on. "That's good. Let me have that bat."

"You don't need bifocals on," Yogi told Phil.

Del Alston was first up and hit a single. The Yankees dugout cheered.

"Alright!" Phil exclaimed.

"Phil Rizzuto... number ten coming up right now!" the announcer exclaimed. Phil walked up to home plate with a big smile, while everyone cheered.

Phil stood at home plate and took some warm up swings.

Yogi Berra's Last Game

The pitcher wound up and threw the ball. Phil tried to bunt but it's a strike.

Del led off first and stole second base.

"That a boy!" Phil shouted. The second pitch is thrown. Phil swung and tried not to break his wrist to prevent a strike. "Did I swing at that?" Phil asked the umpire.

"Yup," the Umpire replied.

"I haven't swung at a ball in years," Phil remarked. He waited for the next pitch as Dell led off second. The Austrian pitcher threw to second base for an error and Del stole third. The ball was thrown to third base for another error. Dell sprinted as Phil stepped out of his way. He slid into home on his knees and raised his arms in victory. Phil cheered with the crowd and stepped back up to home plate with a smile.

The Yankees dugout cheered and the score is 1-0.

"Way to hustle bro!" Bill exclaimed to Del.

"We want you to run!" the dugout shouted to Phil.

"Okay!" Phil shouted. Phil swung at the pitch but it's a strike.

Yogi Berra's Last Game

"They curved me twice!" Phil shouted as he walked off thinking he was out.

"You're not out!" the dugout shouted.

"You've got one more Phil," the announcer said. The umpire held up two fingers as Phil turned around and stood at home plate for the next pitch. The pitch was thrown. Phil swung at the pitch and struck out.

Yogi Berra's Last Game

Phil walked from home plate to the dugout as the crowd cheered for his effort. He took off his batting helmet and put on his Yankees cap.

"Three curve balls!" Phil exclaimed. "Three curve balls he threw me!" Yogi stood with his arms folded in front of the dugout smiling at Phil as he walked towards him.

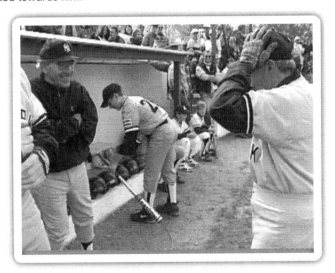

"He hooked you three times," Ron LeFlore said. "Hooked you three times."

"Three times!" Phil exclaimed. "I can't believe it!" Yogi stood beside Phil in front of the dugout listening with a big grin.

"Yeah, three times!" Phil exclaimed. "One fastball and three curves!"

"All right Phil… yah got an RBI!" someone shouted. Yogi looked on with a smile.

"Holy cow!" Phil exclaimed. Yogi stood and laughed. "Unbelievable!" Phil exclaimed. Yogi consoled Phil and patted him on the shoulders.

"We made too many wrong mistakes," Yogi said after losing the 1960 World Series to the Pittsburgh Pirates.

Yogi Berra's Last Game

"Philip, They got the book on you!" Ralph Branca shouted from the dugout. "Three curves, he knew you couldn't t hit the curve!"

"I want to tell yah!" Phil exclaimed as Bill went up to hit. Bill White stood at home plate. The pitch is thrown. He swung at the pitch for a strike.

"Whoa, what a swing he had on that!" Phil exclaimed from the dugout.

"He was going deep," Yogi commented.

"I'm not gonna get on. I can see that," Phil said. "If he's gonna curve me every time." The pitch is thrown and Bill let it go by for a ball. "I think I had a midget bat up there," Phil said. "I tell yah."

"You gotta have your big bat Phil," Yogi said. The pitch was thrown. Bill swung and it's a strike.

"The kids got nice form," Phil commented about Bill's swing. The pitch was thrown and Bill drove it to right field. The Yankees dugout and the crowd cheered! Bill began to run to first but the ball was caught by the

Austrian first baseman.

"Oh... nice play!" Phil exclaimed.

Ron LeFlore went up to bat. The pitch is thrown and it's ball one. He took some practice swings. The pitch is thrown and Ron drives it for a double. The crowd and Yankees dugout cheered. The Austrian catcher threw to second base for an error and Ron ran to third.

"Oh! Homerun... come on!" Phil shouted.

"Inside the park!" someone shouted.

Joe Pignatano walked up to home plate to bat.

"Come on Piggy!" shouted the dugout.

"Who follows Piggy?" Yogi asked. "Who follows Piggy?"

"Tony," someone said.

"Tony... okay. Where the hell's Tony?" Yogi asked as Tony stood up.

"Alright… get up there Tony." The pitch is thrown to Joe. He slammed it to left field for a single and drove in Ron for an RBI. The Yankees dugout cheered with the crowd.

"Yeah… how do yah like that!" Phil exclaimed. "That a boy!"

Tony Veteri, a four-time Super Bowl referee, came up to bat. He hit a grounder to left field but was thrown out at first. The side is retired with the score 2-0 Yankees.

Yogi stood at home plate with Joe catching to check out John's pitching ability for the Yankees. He stood on the mound as Whitey coached him. Whitey ranks first with a winning percentage of .690 among pitchers with at least 300 career decisions. That's the all-time highest percentage in modern baseball history. His career winning percentage cannot be attributed just to being on a good team: The Yankees were

1,486 -1,027 during his 16 years; without his 236 -106, they had 1,250 wins and 921 losses, for a won-loss percentage of .576. Whitey was 11.4 percentage points higher than his team's record, independent of his record. Whitey Ford's 2.75 earned run average is the second-lowest among starting pitchers whose careers began after the advent of the live-ball era in 1920. Clayton Kershaw's current 2.51 ERA is the only pitcher that is lower. Whitey had 45 shutout victories in his career, including eight 1-0 wins.

"Have you pitched before?" I asked.

"Never," John replied. He wound back and threw a pitch.

"They talk about the fall of the Yankees. Well, the Yankees would have fallen a lot sooner if it wasn't for my banty rooster," said Casey Stengel regarding Whitey and the nickname Stengel called him.

Yogi Berra's Last Game

Yogi jumped back as the ball came a little too close to his knees.

Joe began to lunge for the ball as it rolled past him. He stopped short, stood up, stared back at John and threw him the ball. John stepped off the mound and tossed the ball to the Chairman of the Board as he stepped on.

"If Steinbrenner saw you right now you'd get a million and a half," Whitey teased. He looked at the ball and dropped it into his glove the same way he did when he won his tenth World Series game.

"You kind of took it for granted around the Yankees that there was always going to be baseball in October," said Whitey Ford in his book "Slick" published in 1988.

He blew into his pitching hand and reached for the ball. He wrapped his hand around it in the pocket of the glove.

Yogi Berra's Last Game

He placed his fingers strategically on the ball and wound back for his one pitch of the game.

Whitey let it go and threw a strike in his dress shoes.

Yogi Berra's Last Game

"Strike!" Whitey exclaimed as he backed away from the mound. "That's all I can tell yah."

"Alright coach," John replied.

"I forget how to throw the ball around," Phil commented. An Austrian player got a single and led off first to steal second.

"Pick em off John!" Phil shouted. "Pick em off! He's trying to steal! John, quick pitch him! John! Moore quick pitch!" John threw the pitch and the batter hit a grounder to him. John looked at second and then to first. "First," Phil shouted. "First, first!" John threw the ball to Dell at first base and the Austrians are out. The side is retired. "That a boy Moore!" Phil shouted.

Whitey gave Phil him a pat on the back when they walked off the field. "He's a hotdog... I'll tell yah!" Phil exclaimed to Whitey as he walked toward me on his way to the dugout. "You got hit in the leg didn't yah..." Phil said to me.

"Darn right!" I replied as though I had earned some recognition. "I took one for the team!"

"You saved us!" Phil exclaimed. "You saved us a run!" Phil was being kind to me but he raised millions for St. Joeseph's School for the Blind.

"Where's our skipper?" Phil asked as he saw Yogi. "Get somebody to hit for me."

"Who?" Yogi asked.

"One of the young kids," Phil said.

"You wanta hit? Get a uniform on!" Yogi said to me as I filmed him.

"I can't hit a curve," Phil said. "I haven't hit a curve ball in years."

"They got your number," Ralph Branca said from the dugout.

"I know it, they're gonna keep coming," Phil said. "Maybe I'll bat left handed."

"Bunt the damn thing," Bill said. "Bunt it."

"Yeah but I can't. The bats to light," Phil replied.

"I gotta go and hit for us," Yogi said. "Gonna see how it goes."

"Yeah. He threw me three curve balls... not much... but it's like a little slider," Phil said. "What do yah gotta do Yogi?"

"I'm gonna hit for you," Yogi replied.

"Oh... okay," Phil replied. "Good."

"You going out and play second Phil?" Yogi asked.

"No, go and get somebody else to go out there and play second," Phil replied.

"No, you go play second," Bill coaxed.

"No," Phil replied wearily.

John hit a grounder that hopped to third.

"Oh, look at that drive!" Phil shouted. John got a double and Larry rounded third to home for a run. "How do you like Moore? Son of a gun is pitching and hitting!" Phil exclaimed.

"All right Larry!" Bill shouted as he got to the dugout.

"Nice Going Lar!" Phil exclaimed. John knelt at second breathing hard after sprinting for the double. "Look at em. He's kneeling down now at second," Phil commented to Bill as if they were in the broadcast booth of Yankees stadium. "He's gotta be tired on second base. He's kneeling down."

"He's been drinking all night every night," Bill commented.

A short time later Phil handed his glove to one of the Austrian players subbing for the Yankees.

"Here yah are," Phil said. "You take my place."

"I'm gonna hit for Phil," Yogi said as he got ready to head to home plate.

"You gonna be the DH?" Bill asked the Austrian sub for the Yankees.

"DH… designated hitter…" the Austrian player translated.

"You might not play, but you just DH," Bill instructed.

"Are you gonna play second base too?" Phil asked the Austrian player.

"Yeah," the Austrian player replied. Dell hit a drive to center field for a triple and drove John home for a run.

"John Moore comes in!" the announcer exclaimed.

"There's two out," Phil said from the dugout.

Yogi walked to home plate wearing the Yankees cap and road gray uniform he hadn't worn for nearly a decade. He hadn't been to Yankees Stadium, let alone worn a Yankees uniform, since George Steinbrenner dismissed him as manager in the 1985 MLB season. This moment was the beginning of the end for Yogi Berra's exile from the Yankees.

> *Yogi walked to home plate wearing the Yankees cap and road gray uniform he hadn't worn for nearly a decade.*

Yogi Berra's Last Game

The Austrian catcher put on his mask, as arguably the greatest MLB catcher of all time stepped up to home plate. I wondered if he knew this.

Yogi is one of two catchers including Johnny Bench on the All-Century. A panel of experts first compiled a list of the 100 greatest Major League Baseball players from the past century. Over two million fans then voted on the players using paper and online ballots. The team roster includes other Yankees legends like Babe Ruth, Lou Gehrig, and Mickey Mantle. "Baseball is ninety percent mental and the other other half is physical," Yogi once said. He was sixty-nine years old and the other half might not be so dependable, so he would have to rely on the ninety percent. Yogi stood at homeplate waiting for the pitch and took a few warm up swings.

The pitch was thrown and Yogi hit a grounder to left field.

Yogi Berra's Last Game

The crowd cheered as he ran to first base.

"Throw it way!" Bill shouted. "Throw it away!"

"Oh, he got him!" Phil shouted as Yogi was thrown out at first. He ran back to the dugout. Yogi's number eight, which was retired by the Yankees in 1972, could be prominently seen on his Yankees road gray jersey.

Yogi Berra's Last Game

Yogi arrived at the dugout as a discussion of a pitching change began.

"I can't go out there again," John told Phil.

"Yeah," Phil told Bill as he sat next to him on the dugout wall. "He said he needs to find somebody else to pitch."

"We'll find somebody to pitch. Don't throw easy. Don't let them hit off yah!" Bill exclaimed. "We don't want anybody hitting. If we let them hit we're in trouble."

"Why?" Phil asked.

"Because we ain't got nobody who can catch the God damn thing!" Bill half joked.

A short time later Ralph Branca, who coached third base during the game, walked up to me.

"They're a little nervous and we're just finding our gear," Ralph observed. "They'll get some runs. They look pretty good."

A short time later the Austrian's were back up with men on base.

"Uh oh... uh oh!" Bill exclaimed from the dugout.

"Uh... oh!" Phil exclaimed as the Austrian hit a single and drove in a run. "You left two out on third base!" Phil shouted from the dugout. "We're in trouble here."

"Hit the glove... hit the glove!" Bill exclaimed as John pitched a strike."Good!"

"John you can wind up!" Phil shouted. "That a boy!" The Austrian side was retired. Joe walked up to me on his way back to the dugout from catching the inning.

"Three outs in this game that's all," Joe teased. "Three outs each inning. You're out!"

"It's only two strikes." Phil commented to Bill.

"I think you're right," Bill replied. "Two hell with it!"

"That's alright though," Phil said. "We're gonna take it."

267

John Moore walked from the mound to Phil in front of the dugout.

"I thought you were gonna say you only got two strikes on em," Phil said to John as he approached him. "I was gonna kill yah!"

"Did you hear that?" Bob asked Phil.

"What?" Phil asked.

"Larry's telling him, let him hit," Bob replied. Phil looked at him in disbelief as he processed what he'd been told.

"That's why I was..." John began to say in reply to what Phil was told. "And then I was having trouble..."

"No..." Phil replied in lengthy displeasure.

Yogi completely unaware of the conversation walked over to John and Phil.

"You alright?" Yogi asked John referring to his pitching arm. "Let me take you out." Bob walked over to Yogi and whispered into his ear. Yogi looked annoyed as he listened.

"Let em hit it!" Yogi exclaimed angrily. "Bullshit let em hit!"

"Yogi Berra is a wiser man than me." said President Richard Nixon.

"If you're going to cheat, don't get caught," Yogi once said.

"Hey, wait a minute." Bill said as he heard them talking, while resting on the edge of the dugout wall. "What did you... what did I hear you say?"

"Yeah, Karl said let em hit. Let them hit. That was the difference," Larry replied, referring to the runs the Austrian team had just scored. Bill White sat on the wall of the dugout. He pushed his Yankees cap up on his forehead looking a little concerned.

"What?" Bill asked befuddled. "What'd he say?"

"Karl said let them hit the ball," Larry repeated.

"No!" Bill exclaimed indignantly. "We're not gonna let them hit!"

"Alright, do what you want," Larry replied, as if he agreed with Karl.

"We're not... to hell with them! Make them hit the ball! Don't give. Don't let em hit!" Bill exclaimed. "Don't let em hit!" According to this conversation Karl Hofer, the Austrian promoter, was fixing the game to help the Austrian team win. Casinos Austria, a gaming corporation that owns and operates gambling around the globe, was sponsor of the game. Was Karl cheating?

"This the new pitcher?" Phil asked Yogi as he walked past me.

"Yup... new one," Yogi replied as he grinned.

Yogi Berra's Last Game

"I got to get something more to sit on," Phil said as he sat on the cold concrete wall of the dugout. "This is cold here."

Ron Leflore came in to score a run as the game continued on.

"Nice coaching Branca!" Phil shouted. When NL president Bill White saw Karl Hofer standing near the dugout he shouted over to him.

"Hey Karl... Karl... you trying to bribe my pitcher!" Bill exclaimed angrily. "We ain't giving up nothing! We ain't giving up no runs!"

"Is he on our team?" Phil asked as he got a glimpse of the pitching relief. "Is he gonna pitch for us or what?" The 1951 "Shot Heard Round the World" Pennant relief pitcher Ralph Branca approached me. He was born January 6, 1926 and died November 23, 2016 at 90.

"What do you want now a comment?" Ralph asked. "I told yah they'd score some runs and they'll score some more. We got to put you in this game Randy, put the defense in. Cuz I know you can't hit." Ralph teased as he grinned and walked away. I grinned too. It's not every day Brooklyn Dodgers pitching legend Ralph Branca criticizes your batting skills.

"This kid gonna pitch for us or against us?" Phil asked.

"Whatever," the Austrian player replied. "Whatever you like."

"Oh... send em over!" Phil exclaimed. Dell retired the side in the fourth with the score five to four in favor of the Yankees. "We need some runs...runs!" Phil exclaimed.

"You gonna go back in... right Phil," Bob said.

"Maybe," Phil replied.

Whitey came in from the field and grabbed a couple bats. He took several hard swing with the bats to warm up.

"Sooner or later the arm goes bad. It has to... Sooner or later you have to start pitching in pain." Whitey Ford once said.

Yogi Berra's Last Game

"Yogi will sign it," Phil told the fan.

"What… where do I go on here?" Yogi asked as he looked at the ball Phil handed him.

"You can go on cause you got a small name," Phil said. "I couldn't get mine on there." Yogi signed the ball. "Perfect," Phil said as Yogi handed the ball back to the fan with a smile.

"Half the lies they tell about me aren't true." Yogi once said.

"He's hitting a homer when I hit the single," Whitey said, as he stood next to Ron LeFlore in the batting lineup.

"Come on Whitey!" Ron exclaimed. "Let's go!"

"I want to hit the first homerun in Austria!" Whitey exclaimed. He stopped a lot of ballplayers from hitting home runs in their careers and now it was his turn to knock one out.

Meanwhile, Phil sat in the dugout with a choirboy he met a few days before. "How yah doing? When you gonna go back to ah... rehearse?" Phil began to ask. "When you start singing again?"

"Monday," the choirboy replied. Bill sat next to Phil listening.

"Tomorrow," Bill responded. It was Sunday, September 18th.

"You gonna run to first or you want me to take off!" Bob asked Whitey.

"No... you're gonna run," Whitey replied laughing.

"Number sixteen up next... Whitey Ford!" the announcer exclaimed.

Whitey went up to home plate and took a couple warm up swings. The pitch is thrown. He slammed the first pitch towards the American flag in right field. The crowd cheered but it's caught for the out. Whitey pitched a record 22 games; 146 innings; and 94 strikeouts in his World Series career.

"Ha, ha... Lancelotti's running for him," Phil commented about Whitey's pinch runner. "Ha, ha!" Yogi watched from the dugout with a big grin on his

Yogi Berra's Last Game

face as Whitey pulled his helmet off.

"Think! How the hell are you gonna think and hit at the same time?" Yogi said, referring to what was thrown to him as a young Yankees batter.

"Ron LeFlore comes up to bat!" the Announcer exclaimed.

"He said he was gonna hit a homerun," Phil commented from the dugout. The pitch is thrown and the ball hit his shin. Ron hobbled around to ease the pain.

"Oh geez!" Phil exclaimed.

Ron stepped up to home plate and took a warm up swing. The pitch is thrown with two strikes on the count. Ron slammed the ball to center field.

"Oh!" Phil exclaimed as the dugout jumped up and cheered with the crowd. "There it is!" someone exclaimed. "He said he was gonna do it!" Phil exclaimed. Ron flipped the bat into the air and ran the bases with his arms extended like wings. He rounded the bases and gave a high-five to the Austrian players as he ran past them.

"How do yah like that... huh," Phil remarked. "Ha, ha, ha... first homerun!" Ron wiped the dirt off his shoes crossing home plate and took a bow. Yogi congratulated him with a pat on the back, as he managed his last team.

"It ain't like football. You can't make up no trick plays," Yogi once said of his plans for managing the Yankees during the 1964 World Series.

"You said you were gonna do it!" Phil yelled to Ron. "Yah did it... son of a gun... great!"

"Three for three so far," Yogi told Ron referring to his hitting average for the game. Ron gave a fist pump.

"That's right!" Ron exclaimed.

279

"See, what yah gotta do though... is yah gotta take it when he points it and splice it and put it in," a guy commented to Yogi about editing the footage being filmed.

"Ha, ha... when you point it," Yogi said with a grin as he pointed his finger like Babe Ruth did, when he called his shot against the Cubs, in the fifth inning of Game 3 at the 1932 World Series in Chicago's Wrigley Field. The home run was Babe Ruth's fifteenth, and last, in his forty-one post-season games. Yogi shook hands with the "Sultan of Swat" in his rookie year. Yogi has twelve World Series home runs, with one being the first World Series pinch-hit home run. NY Yankees Mickey Mantle has the record at eighteen.

An umpire reportedly told Yogi he was the ugliest player he'd ever seen. He shrugged off the insults in signature fashion."So I'm ugly," Yogi said. "I never saw anyone hit with his face."

Yogi Berra's Last Game

Yogi looked at me. "You got enough film to do that?" he asked.

"Yeah… I do," I replied quickly to go along with the joke

The score was Yankees six and Austrians four in the bottom of the fifth. Whitey covered first base.

The pitch is thrown and the Austrian hit a grounder to Dell. He threw it to third for the out with a man on first.

"What a play!" Phil shouted. "Holy cow!"

Another Austrian hit a ground ball to Yankees substitute player Sal at second base.

"First base… first base!" Whitey shouted.

"Plenty of time!" someone shouted from the dugout. Second base threw it in the dirt to Whitey at first. Whitey lunged and was able to scoop it up but the runner beat the throw and was safe.

"Jeez!" Phil exclaimed.

"Nice throw Sal!" someone shouted sarcastically from the dugout.

"Ha, ha!" Phil laughed.

"We're not bowling here!" someone shouted.

"Way to pick it Whitey!" Ron shouted.

"This the sixth inning?" John asked.

"Fifth!" Phil replied. "Bottom of the fifth."

"Phil you gonna hit again?" Yogi asked.

"For who?" Phil asked. "This the bottom of the fifth."

"We're only going five," Ron said.

"I don't know," Yogi said.

"Two out!" Whitey shouted from first.

"I heard we was going five," someone said.

"That's what I heard," Phil said.

"Larry," Ron said. "Massaroni said five."

Dell threw a pitch and struck out the Austrian hitter.

"Got em!" Phil exclaimed. "Alright!"

"We got more innings?" Yogi asked.

"We're still playing." Phil observed.

"I'd be gassing em. I ain't gonna lighten up on em," Ron said. "Throw em some sliders Yogi. Throw some sliders."

"Let's find out how many innings they're playing Yog," Phil said.

"Karl says we gotta get up one more time," Bob said.

"Why's he telling you... why don't he tell us!" Yogi exclaimed.

"How many innings?" Phil asked.

"How many innings?" Yogi asked.

"Seven," Larry replied.

"Seven!" Yogi exclaimed.

"Seven!" Phil exclaimed.

"What do these guys want? They can't score from there to there," Yogi joked. The Yankees could feel the win was there's.

The player who covered second base earlier in the game and threw the ball in the dirt to Whitey tried to convince Yogi to let him play second again.

"You're finished. Sit down!" Yogi exclaimed as he waved him off with his hands. "He can't even throw to second base!"

The Yankees were to close to winning this game. Yogi was making sure there was no way they were going to lose. He wasn't letting someone screw up and let the Austrians score more runs.

Phil laughed as he sat in the dugout watching him Yogi manage.

"You can throw from second to Whitey at first… can't yah?" Yogi asked Phil, as he looked around the dugout for a player to cover second base in the next inning.

"Yogi who's up?" someone shouted from the dugout.

285

"White!" Phil shouted. "You hit White!"

"Hey White!" Ron shouted. "Let's go!"

"Let Yogi go hit!" Bill shouted with a grin. "Rizzuto you hit!"

"I hit already… Bill go up and hit!" Yogi ordered.

Bill looked out at the mound to see who was pitching for the Austrians.

"Who is he? He doesn't throw slow," Bill commented. "He's a pretty good pitcher."

"Rizzuto… you can bunt!" Ron exclaimed. "You go up to bunt?"

"You got any advice?" I asked Enos, who sat in calmly in the dugout watching the game unfold.

"I see a lot on our side that can be improved!" Enos exclaimed. "Let's play defense! We got the lead now! Let's play defense!"

Over the nineteen years Enos played in the Major Leagues he posted

Yogi Berra's Last Game

a batting average of.300 and 2,383 hits. He might have approached 3000 hits if not for the the three years he served in WWII. He played in ten All Star Games, eight straight with the St. Louis Cardinals from 1946 to 1953. "One of the greatest," remarked Yankees manager Casey Stengel. The Yankees won three pennants and two World Series, with Enos playing, between 1956 and 1958. He hit a three run homer in Game 3 of the 1956 World Series.

"Dell... Dell Alston," Larry shouted. "Where is he?"

"He's got a bad leg," Yogi said as he looked around for a hitter to go up to bat.

"Yogi... we got another player here!" Phil shouted from the dugout. "He can play."

"Can you play shortstop?" Yogi asked.

"Absolutely!" the sub player exclaimed.

"I'll play second," Phil said.

Yogi Berra's Last Game

"Up to bat is Larry Massaroni!" the announcer exclaimed.

The pitch is thrown and Larry hit a grounder for a single.

"Yeah... go ahead," Phil told Yogi.

"I'll go out to second," Yogi said. "Don't want yah. Sit down." Yogi wasn't giving any more thought to who would cover second base.

"You're managing," John said. "You can put yourself anywhere."

"What glove am I gonna use?" Yogi asked as he prepared himself to play second base. He was playing defense for the Yankees once again.

Ralph Branca is third base coach giving Whitey the sign to bunt.

The pitch is thrown and Ford bunts. The catcher threw his mask and lunged for the ball. Whitey stood at home plate watching the ball to see if it would go foul.

"You gave the sign to bunt pal!" Whitey shouted to Ralph at third base. Whitey smiled as he picked up the catcher's mask and handed it to him.

Yogi Berra's Last Game

"No! It's a fowl ball!" Phil shouted from the dugout. Whitey stepped up to home plate as he looked at the umpire.

"Foul ball Whitey!" Phil shouted from the dugout. "Foul ball... foul ball!"

"That's why I didn't run," Whitey told the umpire. Whitey was elected to the Hall of Fame in 1974 and the Yankees retired his number sixteen the same year. The Yankees dedicated a plaque to Whitey in Moument Park at Yankees Stadium in 1987. "The way he got people out, he never gave a guy a pitch to hit in an important moment," Yogi said of Whitey.

Whitey took some warm up swings and stood waiting for another pitch. The pitch is thrown. Whitey hit it to right field for a single and drove in a run for the Yankees. His pinch runner ran to first.

Yogi Berra's Last Game

"Look at this...look at this!" Phil shouted. "Another run!"

"He's a punch and Judy hitter," Yogi teased.

"Oh, big discussions tonight," someone joked. Dell is at bat with a man on first and second.

"One ball... one strike!" the announcer exclaimed. The pitch was thrown and Dell swung for a strike. He stood poised at home plate for the next pitch. The second base runner attempted to steal third but was tagged out.

"Oh, that was a good move!" Phil exclaimed sarcastically. Bob, the pinch runner of Italian lineage and NY tourist, attempted to steal second but was tagged out for a double play.

"Double play!" Phil shouted. "Oh!"

"Can you believe this... punch and Judy hitter!" Dell exclaimed as he walked from home plate to the dugout. "Nice going guys... nice going!"

"Phil!" Whitey exclaimed laughing. "They tricked one of out best Italian base runners."

"You better teach your boy how to run!" someone shouted.

> *"Phil!" Whitey exclaimed laughing. "They tricked one of our best Italian base runners."*
>
> *"You better teach your boy how to run," someone said.*

"Oh jeez!" Phil exclaimed.

"Double... double steal!" Larry exclaimed. "They got em both!"

"With our big power hitter up there!" Phil remarked referring to Dell.

"Two Italians," someone joked.

"Oh shit!" Larry recalled. "I'm pitching... aw damn!"

"Are yah?" Phil asked.

The Yankees were out and third base coach Ralph Branca walked up to me on his way back to the dugout.

"You know some guys are uncoachable. Bad, very bad play," Ralph said half joking. "Make me look bad after I did a wonderful brainy job of having a hit and run and scoring a man from second."

The Yankees took the field with Yogi playing second and Whitey playing first. The pitch is thrown and the Austrian hitter drove it for a triple.

"Hey!" Bill shouted.

"Whoa!" Phil shouted. The pitch is thrown. The Austrian hit a grounder and ran to first. Dell scooped up the grounder and threw it to Whitey at first for the out. The greatest Yankees pitcher wasn't a bad first baseman.

"I don't care what the situation was, how high the stakes were – the bases could be loaded and the pennant riding on every pitch, it never bothered Whitey," said Mickey Mantle. "He pitched his game." Mickey, Whitey and Yogi powered the Yankee Dynasty that produced 14 American League pennants and nine World Series titles from 1949-64. At the heart of baseball's greatest dynasty was Whitey Ford. He won a higher percentage of his decisions than any other modern pitcher.

294   Yogi Berra's Last Game

"All right Whitey!" Bill exclaimed.

"You see him lift that foot off the bag… son of a gun!" Phil exclaimed.

295

It's not often you see Whitey Ford playing first base and Yogi Berra playing second base, side by side.

"Look at Yogi playing in," Bill commented from the dugout.

Yogi Berra's Last Game

Dell struck out the next hitter.

"All right Dell!" Bill exclaimed. The pitch is thrown and the batter hit a grounder to left field and drove in another run for the Austrians.

"Uh oh," Bill shouted from the dugout.

"Oh what a bad hop that was!" Phil exclaimed from the dugout.

"Two outs," Bill said. Yogi covered second base with one out left in the inning. Yogi also played 260 games in the outfield, two games at first base, and one game at third in the 19 years he played for the Yankees. Yogi always wanted to do what was best for the team. The only time he played second base in a competitive ballgame was this moment in 1994.

"One time I didn't run a ball out full speed, Joe got ahold of me, and let's just say, it never happened again," Yogi said of Dimaggio.

"Seeing him for the first time, best-looking ballplayer I ever saw, and eventually my great pal," Yogi said of teammate Mickey Mantle who could bat left or right handed. "He hits from both sides of the plate. He's amphibious."

"Two outs!" Phil shouted as a very tall Austrian player stepped up to bat. "Where did this guy come from?"

"Oh Jesus Christ!" Bill exclaimed.

"Yeah!" Phil exclaimed.

"Big strike zone!" Whitey shouted unfazed. "Big strike zone!"

The pitch is thrown and the Austrian player drove it deep to left field.

"Oh!" Phil shouted.

"He ain't gonna catch it that's the problem," Bill commented. "Is he?"

Bill White condemned racism in baseball, although he acknowledged that even as National League president, he couldn't do much to prevent it.

Yogi Berra's Last Game

The outfielder caught it. The side is retired and the Yankees are back up to hit.

"Whoa!" Phil exclaimed. "Holy cow!"

"That's a big fella!" Bill exclaimed.

"He is big," Phil remarked.

Yogi walked into the dugout area after playing second base.

"Good job Yog!" Whitey shouted.

"That's it... I'm finished," Yogi said. "Who's got my coat?" Yogi turned around and Bill tossed his coat to him. "Ah, here we go," Yogi said as he caught it. "I'm finsihed. I played my one inning."

"We won a lot before that, so for me it wasn't that bad, somebody has to win. Yes, I knew it was gone," Yogi said of Pittsburgh Pirates Bill Mazeroski's Game 7 winning home run in the 1960 World Series. Yogi hit a home run in Game 7 that gave the Yankees their first lead, 5-4 but the Pirates won 10-9. Mantle hit three home runs in the series. "We made too many wrong mistakes," said Yogi of the Yankees 1960 World Series loss.

Yogi Berra's Last Game

I'm too stiff, Phil said, bundled up in his coat. "LeFlore is gonna hit."

"You're up first," Larry said.

"Huh... after me," Phil said as he's handed a bat. "No, that's too small. I gotta get a bigger bat." Phil searched through the bats for one that would work for him. "I'm leading off. Whoa, that ones a... that's a good bat there." Phil remarked as he examined the bat and walked to the on-deck circle to warm up. "Oh wait a minute!" Phil exclaimed when he saw the pitcher on the mound. "I'm not batting against that guy!"

Ron LeFlore stood waiting to hit. He was a center fielder who stole 455 bases in his career with a .288 batting average. Ron was the stolen base leader in 1978 and 1980. Detroit Manager Billy Martin helped Ron get paroled from Jackson State prison to try out for the Tigers in 1973. LeFlore was an American League All-Star selection in 1976 finishing the season with a .316 batting average and 58 stolen bases.

Dell went up to hit and Phil signed more autographs in the dugout.

"You don't have that other kinda pen... huh? The soft point pen... no?" Phil asked. "We got to get that other kind. Oh, here we are." The pitch is thrown and Dell popped up in center field for the out. Ron LeFlore went up to bat. The pitch is thrown and he hit a line drive to right field for a single.

Seventy-eight year old Hall of Fame great Enos Slaughter walked aggressively to home plate. During his MLB career he was renowned for his smooth swing that made him a reliable contact hitter. He was a World Series Champion four times. During his nineteen year career he had 1,304 RBI'; and 169 home runs in 2,380 games played.

"Scooter your up," someone said in the dugout. "Got a man on."

"No, Slaughter's gonna hit," Phil replied. Slaughter replaced Phil

Yogi Berra's Last Game

Rizuto on the Yankees roster August 25, 1956.

"You're up Phil," shouted someone.

"Slaughter's up," Phil replied. "Oh, there's two out."

"There's one out," someone replied.

Enos picked up the bat from the last hitter and threw it out of his way on the way to home plate. When he returned from his military service in 1946, he led the National League with 130 RBI. His hustle helped the St. Louis Cardinals to a World Series win over Ted Williams and the Red Sox.

Enos retired from baseball after the 1959 season and was elected to the Baseball Hall of Fame.

"My life is complete now," Slaughter explained to reporters. "I was never bitter before, but I was disappointed."

"This is my first time today," Enos told the umpire and catcher as he stepped up to home plate. He took a few warm up swings.

"Phil's getting up next," someone said in the dugout.

"No that guys gonna hit. Yah gotta let that guy hit next," Phil explained. "He'll get on… then I'll get up. He came over and helped us out."

Ron stole second base and third off an error when the ball was thrown over the second baseman. The dugout cheered with Enos at home plate and Ron on third. The pitch was thrown. Enos hit a line drive to left field for a single. He drove in Ron for the last RBI he would ever hit in his baseball career.

"The thing I remember," Stan Musial said of Slaughter, "was him scoring that run in the seventh game of the 1946 World Series."

Yogi Berra's Last Game

Enos took off for first base, but his diminished reflexes caught up with the enthusiasm a hit can bring. The pinch runner ran to first for Enos and Ron ran home.

The crowd cheered and surrounded Enos as he approached the dugout. Meanwhile, the other players tried to talk Phil into hitting.

"Come on, get out there. You have to do it," someone coaxed Phil. "You gotta get that hit."

"No, no... I'm good," Phil replied as he pointed to the other player. "He's up."

"You're up kid," someone said.

"No, no... he's up," Phil replied.

"There's still one out," someone said.

"You're not out of this Rizzuto," another insisted.

Enos stood trapped amongst the crowd of fans signing autographs. He struggled to get back to the dugout to sit down and rest his legs.

"Let me go sit down... let me sit down," Enos said. He handed back an autographed baseball to a kid. "I'd rather sit down, I had to run!" There was no "Mad Dash" today, but he will always will be a Hall of Fame legend.

Whitey made his way through the crowd to his old teammate Enos. He put his arm around Enos's shoulder and patted him on the back.

"Enos!" Whitey exclaimed. "The oldest guy to ever get a hit in Austria!" Whitey laughed with Enos as he congratulated him. That was the last hit of his incredible major league baseball career.

"Let's get over here and sit down," Enos insisted as he autographed another ball. "Things would be better."

Yogi Berra's Last Game

"Enos, are you going to do a little partying tonight?" I joked.

"No... nope!" Enos exclaimed with a smile. He looked up at me from autographing a ball. "That's the first time I come through in the clutch," Enos joked. "I'm going over and sittin down boys. Let's sit down... be a lot easier."

"Look, they hit him again, you gotta be kiddin!" Phil commented about the pitcher. "I'm not going up there."

"Come on Phil," someone said.

"He just hit that guy three times. Let this kid hit!" Phil exclaimed. "Go ahead. If he gets on, then I'll hit."

"There's still only one out," someone said.

"You want him to hit?" Yogi asked Phil.

"Yeah, that's right," Phil replied. "Look at this guy. I don't like the way he throws."

"If the ball comes inside you better not go in there," Bill commented.

"No, I know it," Phil said. "Look at that. That kid had a nice swing at that!" Bill White went up to home plate. "If White gets on I'll hit," Phil said as the pitch is thrown. Bill slammed the ball to right field for a single and drove in a runner.

"There it is," someone said to Phil. "Let's go!"

"Phil Rizzuto coming up!" the announcer exclaimed. Seventy-seven year old Phil Rizzuto stepped up to home plate.

"Oh gee, this guys to big!" Phil exclaimed as he stared at the pitcher.

"Man on first! Man on third!" the announcer exclaimed. "Ball two!"

"Two, I can't wait!" Phil exclaimed. "I can't wait."

"Two and one!" the announcer exclaimed. "Two balls one strike!" The pitch was thrown and Phil hit a grounder to left field.

"Hell of a player. He won the MVP ahead of me in '50, and it was the best year of my career," Yogi said of his lifetime teammate Phil Rizzuto.

Yogi Berra's Last Game

He ran to first as he drove in a run and got his second RBI of the day for the Yankees.

Phil walked back to the dugout as his pinch runner took his place at first. "Who says the bat doesn't sting... huh... holy cow!" Phil exclaimed.

"Two outs!" Whitey shouted.

"You're cracking it out there," I told Phil as he approached me.

"Yeah. Cracking it out there." Phil replied modestly. "I almost broke my finger on that one." Phil stood for moment, pondering the hit he got, as he examined his finger. "It is three out... right? Well, we got to hold them in now. How many run lead we got? Where's the score?" Phil asked.

"Ten to four!" someone shouted.

"Ten to four. That's enough runs," Bill remarked. "You don't want to lose." This game meant more to these guys than they had let on. They were proud of what they had done that day even as the MLB strike cast a dark shadow on their beloved game. They weren't about to lose now.

A short time later, Phil stood near the dugout and hummed Frank Sinatra's "My Way" as it played over the loudspeaker throughout the field. I walked over to Whitey as he covered first base. "My Way" continued to play with the score ten to four.

"Don't give up seven runs now!" Whitey shouted to Joe at second base as they both laughed.

Casey Stengel's controversial decision not to start Whitey in Games 1 and 4 of the 1960 World Series resulted in the combination of four close games and may have been one reason the Yankees lost to the Pirates.

Whitey walked over when he noticed me standing near first base and spread his arms wide open. "Isn't life wonderful folks!" Whitey cheerfully exclaimed. "Austria on a Sunday afternoon! We're beating the Austrians ten to four and we're having a lot of fun!"

Yogi Berra's Last Game

He began to walk away but stopped and turned around. "And... Frank Sinatra's singing!" Whitey exclaimed as he laughed.

Whitey hustled over to cover first base like a man much younger than his sixty-five years would suggest.

Meanwhile, Bill and Phil sat in the dugout talking to the choirboy they met earlier in the week.

"How do you like the kids form?" Bill asked.

"Kids got a nice arm," Phil replied. "He said he got called out."

"No," Bill replied.

"That's what they told me," Phil said. "I got him in the dugout here cause Karl was kicking him out of the dugout."

"Karl was?" Bill asked befuddled. "For What?"

"Yeah," Phil replied. "Because he didn't want anybody sitting in the dugout except ballplayers."

"He plays ball," Bill remarked.

"He's a ballplayer," Phil agreed. "I know it!"

At the same time, Dell wound up and threw a pitch to the Austrian. He swung and hit a grounder inside the first base line towards Whitey.

Yogi Berra's Last Game

"Uh oh!" Whitey exclaimed as he dropped the grounder he scrambled to scoop up. "Oh!" Whitey groaned as he lunged to retrieve the ball on the first baseline. Del sprinted from the pitchers mound to cover first base.

"How old are you?" Bill asked the choirboy as they sat with Phil in the dugout.

"Fourteen," the choirboy said.

"Fourteen" Bill replied. "Then this could be your last year then."

"Yeah," the choirboy replied.

"Ah... Your voice is getting too low," Bill commented. The choirboy laughed. Whitey tossed the ball to Dell as he ran beat the runner to first .

Whitey gave Dell a congratulatory slap on the back after he tagged out the much younger Austrian player.

"Okay bro!" Whitey shouted to Dell! The crowd cheered. Whitey was the Yankees World Series Game One pitcher in 1955, 1956, 1957, 1958, 1961, 1962, 1963, and 1964. He is the only pitcher in World Series history to start four consecutive Game Ones. He did this twice. Whitey appeared on eight American League All-Star teams between 1954 and 1964. In the 1960 World Series against the Pirates he won Games 3 and 6 with game shutouts. He won twenty five games in 1961 and twenty-four games in 1963.

Yogi Berra's Last Game

"All right!" Bill shouted from the dugout.

"Nice play!" Phil shouted from the dugout.

The next hitter is at bat for the Austrians. The pitch is thrown and the Austrian drove a grounder to right field.

"Oh God!" Whitey exclaimed. The right fielder scooped up the ball and threw it to second. The score is ten to four with a man on first. "Think it over bro," Whitey shouted to the Dell. The pitch is thrown. The Austrian hit it to center field and drove in a run. The score is ten to five with a man on second.

"Don't curve em!" Whitey shouted. "Don't curve em!" Whitey had shoulder surgery in August 1966 and in May 1967 lasted one inning in his his final start. He retired at the age of 38.

"You would be amazed how many important outs you can get by working the count to where the hitter is sure you're going to throw to his weakness and then throw to his power instead." Whitey Ford once said.

The pitch was thrown and the Austrian hit a foul ball. "Oh! What a punch and Judy hitter!" Whitey shouted from first.

Meanwhile, Phil could be heard humming a song during the last out of the final inning.

"We're not taking the trophy home?" a guy asked Phil.

"No." Phil replied.

"We brought it all the way from Brooklyn," the guy said.

"Oh yeah, no way," Phil said. "I don't blame yah."

"So maybe we'll have you hand it to them," the guy said.

"Yeah, if you want me to do it," Phil replied.

Whitey looked down at his shoe's as he covered first.

"I don't know what shoes I'm gonna wear tonight!" Whitey shouted to Joe at second. "I got my best ones on!" Whitey walked towards Joe at second. "Joe!" Whitey shouted. "I got my Florsheim's on!"

Yogi Berra's Last Game

"Whitey!" Joe shouted back. "When you get off the elevator they got a shoeshine shop right there!"

Whitey observed home plate as the pitch was thrown.

The Austrian hit a grounder to Dell. He threw the ball to Whitey at first base.

"He's out!" the umpire shouted as Whitey tagged first base and the runner for the last out of the game.

Yogi Berra's Last Game

Whitey tossed the ball to the umpire. He shook hands with the Austrian player he tagged out and gave him a pat on the back. He waved goodbye to the others on the field and made his way to the dugout.

Ralph Branca stood among the crowd and signed autographs for the fans after the game.

"What was the final score?" Ralph asked me.

"Ten to…" I began to reply as a joke from Ralph was on the way.

"Ten to six… very good!" Ralph replied before I could answer. "We kicked a field goal and made the extra point. They miss the extra point?" Ralph winked and walked away. He was a right handed pitcher with a win-loss record of 88-68; 3.79 ERA; 829 strikeouts in 1,484 innings pitched and was a three time All-Star 1947-1949. Ralph stood on the field beside Jackie Robinson for his first MLB game on Opening Day in 1947.

"Take care," Yogi said to the Austrian players as he made his way to the trophy ceremony.

"Whitey! Whitey get those guys over here!" Joe shouted.

"We got to get everybody over to shake hands," Bill said.

"Alright… we're going out!" Phil shouted. Yogi walked quickly to the trophy ceremony to shake hands with the Austrian players.

Yogi Berra's Last Game

"Don't be running!" Enos exclaimed as he and Phil caught up to Yogi.

"You're the manager," Joe explained. "You gotta except the trophy."

"No, they're getting the trophy," Yogi told Joe.

"They get the trophy!" Phil shouted to Joe.

"Oh, they get the trophy," Joe replied.

"Get over there!" Yogi ordered Joe as he grabbed him by the arm and pushed him ahead of himself.

Yogi grinned as he was able to find his guinea pig to give the trophy to the Austrians and avoid giving a speech.

Yogi Berra's Last Game

"He's giving it out," Yogi said as he pointed to the guy walking toward them with the trophy.

"Let Pignatano present it," Phil said again.

"He can speak it," Enos said.

"He can speak it," Yogi said, referring to Joe's supposed bilingual capabilities to speak the German language. Yogi and Enos had both fought the Nazi's in the second World War but couldn't speak it. Joe took the trophy and stood out in front of the players.

"Do you need a microphone?" someone asked Joe.

"Microphone, for what? They ain't gonna understand me!" Joe exclaimed referring to the Austrian crowds language barrier. Yogi laughed as he removed his Yankees cap and scratched his head. Whitey sucked in his stomach, pulled up his pants and tucked in his shirt. Joe stood for a brief moment looking at the trophy and pondered what he would say. "Guys!" Joe exclaimed. He walked toward the Austrian players carrying the trophy known as the Austrian Cup. "Hey, we enjoyed it… and on behalf of us… and whoever gave this. This is great! Display it, enjoy it, and have fun!" Joe exclaimed.

Joe handed the trophy to the Austrian captain.

"Thank you," the Austrian captain said. He lifted it above his head and everyone applauded and cheered.

"If the people don't want to come out to the ballpark, nobody's going to stop them," Yogi once said. Baseball fans filled the bleachers at Yogi's last competitive game.

Yogi Berra's Last Game

"Yeah Piggy... that a boy!" Phil exclaimed.

"That's the cup," Yogi told the old Yankees as they lined up to high five and shake hands with the Austrian players. The young Austrian ballplayers past by each of the old Yankees.

"MVP," Whitey teased as he high-fived an Austrian player. The next Austrian player walked up. "MVP?" the player asked. "MVP...no," Whitey teased. "No MVP." Yogi heard Whitey and laughed as they stood greeting more players. Yogi, Whitey and Phil knew what it took and what it felt like to be an MVP in the MLB. Phil was in 1950. Yogi was in 1951, 1954 and 1955. Whitey was in 1961.

"In theory, there is no difference between theory and practice. But in practice, there is." Yogi once said.

"Congratulations, thank you, thank you!" Phil exclaimed with a smile as he greeted each Austrian player and shook hands. "The kids were great!"

Yogi Berra's Last Game

"How many more?" Enos asked. The line of Austrian players wasn't ending soon enough for Enos and his aching old legs.

Dell began to walk past Yogi and Whitey in the lineup to greet the Austrian players.

"Hey Dell, wait back, they're gonna come to us!" Yogi ordered. "Let em come to us!"

It was much easier for young Austrian ballplayer legs to walk to Yogi, Whitey, Phil and Enos than their old Hall of Fame legs walking to them. Yogi and Whitey stood in place giving high fives, shaking hands, saying thanks and laughing with each Austrian ballplayer.

"Funny thing about those jokes," Berra told Sport magazine. "When the fans do it, I like it. When the newspaper fellows do it, I like it. I like it when they get on me. Makes me want to do better. Know what I mean? If I get a hit, it's that much better a hit. I figure if they didn't like me, they wouldn't holler. It's when they stop joking with me I'm in trouble."

Yogi Berra's Last Game

"Let em come to us," Yogi said.

Yogi Berra was born on May 12, 1925 and passed away September 22, 2015 at the age of 90 years old while this book was assembled.

"He was the guy who made the Yankees almost seem human," said Mickey Mantle.

I was fortunately given the opportunity to show Yogi a movie trailer, that will become a movie, created from the hours of footage we filmed September 12-18, 1994, this book is created from, at the Yogi Berra Museum and Learning Center August 21, 2011. He smiled and laughed.

"Thank you," Yogi said, as he shook my hand.

Yogi once said, "I really didn't say everything I said." But he did say thank you.

The End

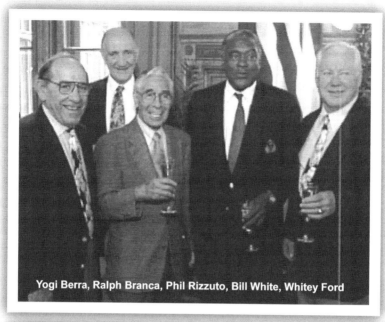

Yogi Berra, Ralph Branca, Phil Rizzuto, Bill White, Whitey Ford

Author Randy Reynolds
filming Phil Rizzuto

336   Yogi Berra's Last Game

50345527R00188

Made in the USA
San Bernardino, CA
20 June 2017